THE IMPORTANCE OF

Mark Twain

by
Skip Press

Lucent Books, P.O. Box 289011, San Diego, CA 92198-9011

These and other titles are included in The Importance Of biography series:

Cleopatra

Christopher Columbus

Marie Curie

Thomas Edison

Albert Einstein

Benjamin Franklin

Galileo Galilei

Thomas Jefferson

Chief Joseph

Malcolm X

Margaret Mead

Michelangelo

Wolfgang Amadeus Mozart

Napoleon Bonaparte

Richard M. Nixon

Jackie Robinson

Anwar Sadat

Margaret Sanger

Mark Twain

H.G. Wells

Dedication

To my wife Debbie, whose magnificence of being would make her my favorite person in any lifetime. Wheresoever she is, *there* is heaven.

Library of Congress Cataloging-in-Publication Data

Press, Skip, 1950-
    Mark Twain / by Skip Press
        p. cm.—(The Importance of)
    Includes bibliographical references (p.) and index.
Summary: Discusses the life, works, and legacy of Mark Twain, the most successful author of his day.
    ISBN 1-56006-043-3 (alk. paper)
    1. Twain, Mark, 1835-1910—Biography—Juvenile literature.
2. Authors, American—19th century—Biography—Juvenile literature. [1. Twain, Mark, 1835-1910. 2. Authors, American.] I.Title. II. Series.
PS1331.P68   1994
818'.409—dc20   93-1827
[B]   CIP
                                                                        AC

Copyright 1994 by Lucent Books, Inc., P.O. Box 289011, San Diego, California, 92198-9011

Printed in the U.S.A.

Contents

Foreword

THE IMPORTANCE OF biography series deals with individuals who have made a unique contribution to history. The editors of the series have deliberately chosen to cast a wide net and include people from all fields of endeavor. Individuals from politics, music, art, literature, philosophy, science, sports, and religion are all represented. In addition, the editors did not restrict the series to individuals whose accomplishments have helped change the course of history. Of necessity, this criterion would have eliminated many whose contribution was great, though limited. Charles Darwin, for example, was responsible for radically altering the scientific view of the natural history of the world. His achievements continue to impact the study of science today. Others, such as Chief Joseph of the Nez Percé, played a pivotal role in the history of their own people. While Joseph's influence does not extend much beyond the Nez Percé, his nonviolent resistance to white expansion and his continuing role in protecting his tribe and his homeland remain an inspiration to all.

These biographies are more than factual chronicles. Each volume attempts to emphasize an individual's contributions both in his or her own time and for posterity. For example, the voyages of Christopher Columbus opened the way to European colonization of the New World. Unquestionably, his encounter with the New World brought monumental changes to both Europe and the Americas in his day. Today, however, the broader impact of Columbus's voyages is being critically scrutinized. *Christopher Columbus,* as well as every biography in The Importance Of series, includes and evaluates the most recent scholarship available on each subject.

Each author includes a wide variety of primary and secondary source quotations to document and substantiate his or her work. All quotes are footnoted to show readers exactly how and where biographers derive their information, as well as provide stepping stones to further research. These quotations enliven the text by giving readers eyewitness views of the life and times of each individual covered in The Importance Of series.

Finally, each volume is enhanced by photographs, bibliographies, chronologies, and comprehensive indexes. For both the casual reader and the student engaged in research, The Importance Of biographies will be a fascinating adventure into the lives of people who have helped shape humanity's past, present, and will continue to shape its future.

Important Dates in the Life of Mark Twain

Samuel Langhorne Clemens born in Florida, Missouri.	**1835**	
		Father dies; works as printer's apprentice.
First nationally published articles appear in the *Saturday Evening Post*.	**1847**	
	1851	Begins training to become steamboat pilot.
	1857	
Brother Henry dies.	**1858**	Deserts Confederate army; travels to Nevada Territory.
First uses the pen name of Mark Twain.	**1861**	
	1863	Publishes "Jim Smiley and His Jumping Frog"; gains national literary fame.
Gives first sold-out lecture in San Francisco.	**1865**	
	1866	
	1868	Makes a living as a traveling lecturer.
Publishes *The Innocents Abroad*.	**1869**	
Publishes *Roughing It*. Daughter Susy born in March; son Langdon dies in June.	**1870**	Marries heiress Olivia Langdon; moves to Buffalo, New York. Son Langdon born.
	1872	
	1874	
Publishes *The Adventures of Tom Sawyer*, an immediate hit.	**1876**	Moves into nineteen-room mansion in Hartford, Connecticut. Daughter Clara born in June.
	1880	
Publishes *The Prince and the Pauper*, his first historical novel.	**1881**	Daughter Jane is born.
	1883	Publishes *Life on the Mississippi*.
Starts publishing company with relative Charles L. Webster. Publishes *The Adventures of Huckleberry Finn*.	**1884**	
	1885	Publishes Ulysses S. Grant's *Memoirs*.
	1888	
Awarded master of arts degree from Yale University.	**1889**	Publishes *A Connecticut Yankee in King Arthur's Court*.
Twain's publishing company goes bankrupt.	**1894**	
	1895	Gives around-the-world lecture tour and pays off all his debts.
	1896	
Favorite daughter Susy dies. Publishes *Personal Recollections of Joan of Arc*.	**1901**	Awarded honorary doctor of letters degree by Yale University.
	1902	
Awarded honorary doctor of letters degree by University of Missouri.	**1904**	Wife Olivia dies.
	1906	
Gives farewell lecture at Carnegie Hall, New York City.	**1907–1908**	Dictates biography to Albert Bigelow Paine.
	1909	
Daughter Jane dies.	**1910**	Mark Twain dies.

The Most Recognized Man in America

At the beginning of the twentieth century, probably no person was more instantly recognized than Samuel Langhorne Clemens, who wrote under the pen name Mark Twain. His wild white hair, bushy eyebrows, thick white mustache, and white linen suit made him easy to spot in any crowd. Indeed, a crowd usually surrounded him. Mark Twain was the most successful American author of his day, a wonderful storyteller, and an expert at selling himself to the public. His books and lecture tours—which were more like stand-up comedy routines than actual lectures—made him a rich man more than once.

Twain's celebrity allowed him to meet the most influential people in the world, particularly in American industry and society. For example, Nikola Tesla, the discoverer of the alternating current and inventor of the electric motor, was a close friend, as was Andrew Carnegie, the founder of U.S. Steel. Twain may also have been the first celebrity ever filmed by a motion picture camera, at Thomas Edison's Long Island, New York, estate.

Twain's popularity stemmed from the fact the he knew his public and intentionally wrote to reach as many people as possible. His writing, he said, was like water, while other writers' works were like fine wine. "A lot more people drink water," he joked.

Twain's major attraction as a writer was his cutting and accurate humorous commentary on life in general. That Twain was able to use and keep his sense of humor is surprising, considering how many disappointments he sustained in

Mark Twain used his keen sense of humor to create colorful tales that generations of readers have enjoyed.

An illustration from one of Twain's most famous novels, The Adventures of Huckleberry Finn. *While some consider* Huckleberry Finn *controversial, Ernest Hemingway praised it as one of the finest novels ever written.*

life. The tragic early demise of his favorite brother, the death of a young son at the age of four, the loss of his most beloved daughter Susy at twenty-four years of age, and the passing of his wife Olivia ("Livy"), whom he worshiped, were crippling emotional blows. Twain somehow overcame all these setbacks, with little loss to his creative genius. In fact, his ability to bounce back from personal loss was astonishing. When almost sixty years old, nearly penniless from bad business decisions, he embarked on a world lecture tour that paid off all his massive debts and made him a wealthy man all over again. This accomplishment made him, perhaps, the first "comeback kid" ever to stimulate the American public imagination.

Many of his books are considered classics now, while at least one is still considered controversial by some: Twain's novel *The Adventures of Huckleberry Finn* was banned from some high schools in the 1980s as racist.

Many writers have acknowledged Twain's genius. American author and Nobel Prize-winner Ernest Hemingway felt that *all* American fiction was influenced by *The Adventures of Huckleberry Finn.* Hemingway called the book the finest American novel ever written.

Someday an American author and entertainer may come along who will have a broader and more lasting influence on the world than Mark Twain, but it has not yet happened. Twain still reigns supreme as the dean of American letters, and his image remains instantly recognizable by people not only in America, but also around the world.

1 In with the Comet

It is a strange coincidence that Mark Twain was born while Halley's Comet was in the North American sky and that he died upon its return, seventy-five years later, just as he had predicted. He was born Samuel Langhorne Clemens, on November 30, 1835, in the small town of Florida, Missouri, to Jane and John Marshall Clemens. Little Sam came two months prematurely. When he arrived, Orion was ten years old, Pamela eight, Margaret seven, and Benjamin three. The new baby was named Samuel after his grandfather on his father's side, and Langhorne after one of his father's friends from Virginia.

John Clemens was a lawyer and shopkeeper. He was a tall man, thin and unusually pale, who looked older than his thirty-six years. His deep-set gray eyes revealed a

Samuel Langhorne Clemens spent his young, formative years in this house in the small town of Florida, Missouri.

fearless nature. One story about his legendary daring was that while at church, he handed the minister a notice about the loss of his cow to be read from the pulpit on Sunday morning. When the minister forgot about the notice, John went to the front of the church and read the note to the congregation himself. Perhaps his father's courage rubbed off on young Sam, who never seemed afraid to try anything.

Mark Twain described his father as "Silent, austere, of perfect probity [high ideals] and high principle; ungentle of manner toward his children, but always a gentleman in his phrasing—and never punished them—a look was enough, and more than enough."[1] Sadly, Twain said that he never remembered seeing or hearing his father laugh.

In contrast to his father's stern disposition, Twain described his mother, Jane, as having "the heart of a young girl." When she was being courted by John Clemens, Jane Lampton was reputed to have been the best dancer in all of Kentucky and was celebrated for her beauty, grace, and wit. "She was of a sunshiny disposition," her son wrote, "and her long life was mainly a holiday to her."[2]

Twain remained close to his mother throughout her life. As a boy, though, he gave her a fair share of worries. Late in her life they had this conversation about his childhood:

> "You gave me more uneasiness than any child I had," she said. "I suppose you were afraid I wouldn't live," he suggested. "No; afraid you *would*!" she joked.[3]

In his early years Sam was a frail child, and his mother was constantly feeding him cod liver oil and home remedies to improve his health. The doctor was summoned for him often. Once Sam caught measles on purpose (probably to get attention), and the family thought he was going to die.

Sam was also an independent and strong-willed child who ran away from home often. In these ways Sam closely resembled Twain's later character Tom Sawyer.

Down on the Farm

Jane Lampton Clemens's brother, John Quarles, had a farm near Florida, Missouri, which was a source of delight for young Sam. Even after the family moved away from Florida, his mother would bring him to the farm every summer. At the farm Sam played with Tabitha, a cousin his own age, whom he called Puss. A slave girl named Mary attended the children, but she was only six years older, so she was more like a playmate. The children spent their days wading in a wide brook with deep pools, playing on swings hung from trees in the pasture, and picking their fill of the blackberries that grew wild along the fences. Just beyond the apple and peach orchards were the slave quarters, where the children visited daily with a white-haired old black woman who told them stories of how to ward off spells and witches. She claimed to be a thousand years old and to have talked with Moses himself. In fact, she said that the bald spot on her head came from fright when she saw the pharaoh drown.

Sam's favorite black person on the farm, however, was a slave named Uncle Dan'l (Daniel). Kind-hearted and dependable, Dan'l became the model for Jim in *Huckleberry Finn.*

Days on Uncle John's farm were heavenly for young Sam. Evenings brought lavish Southern meals of homegrown vegetables and wild game and stories shared around the dinner table. On breezy summer nights the family dined in an outdoor pavilion. As fall approached and the evenings grew chilly, they gathered around the wide, blazing fireplace inside the two-story house. Musical entertainment, group singing, and stories were the main forms of entertainment. The storytelling atmosphere no doubt went a long way toward influencing young Sam to become a teller of tales.

The young Sam, independent and strong-willed, resembled the character of Tom Sawyer (pictured).

Hannibal and the River

In 1839 John Clemens moved his family forty miles east of Florida, Missouri, to the town of Hannibal. Their relocation was probably hastened by the death of Sam's sister Margaret, at the age of nine, from "bilious fever." Moving from the location of her death may have helped the family forget their loss somewhat.

Hannibal was serene and beautiful. It was circled with bluffs like Holliday's Hill on the north and Lover's Leap on the south. It was also a port on the Mississippi River, and the steamboat traffic passing by the town excited young Sam. "When I was a boy," he said in *Life on the Mississippi,* "there was but one permanent ambition among my comrades. That was to be a steamboatman."[4]

Perhaps because of its beauty and importance as a river port, Hannibal's citizens considered their town second only to St. Louis among Missouri towns. It was just a village, but a big city compared to Florida, and it exposed Sam to aspects of society he hadn't seen before.

In Hannibal John Clemens became a jack-of-all-trades, keeping store, serving as justice of the peace, president of the Library Association, and chairman of the Committee on Roads. He also practiced law. John had many professions, not because he was overly ambitious, but because he had to do many things simply to try to make a living. John's ultimate plan, however, was to become rich.

Before coming to Missouri he and his family had lived in Fentress County, Tennessee, where he acquired seventy-five thousand acres of land for about a penny an acre. He hoped to mine the land for coal, copper, or iron, but that never happened. In the Clemens family "the Tennessee land" was a constant source of discussion but never produced a penny. Twain later dramatized the family's hopes for the land in his book *The American Claimant*, but the only profits Sam saw from this land were from writing about it in the novel; he made scarcely a penny from any inheritance. His father's unfulfilled dreams regarding the land prompted him to comment:

It is good to begin life poor; it is good to begin life rich—these are wholesome; but to begin it poor and *prospectively* rich! The man who has not experienced it cannot imagine the curse of it.[5]

A Real Tom Sawyer Adventure

Steamboats are forever associated with the writings of Mark Twain. As a boy, Twain longed to travel on the great ships, and one day he smuggled himself aboard as Albert Bigelow Paine relates in Mark Twain, A Biography:

"One day, when the big packet [steamboat] came down and stopped at Hannibal, [Sam] slipped aboard and crept under one of the boats on the upper deck. Presently the signal-bells rang, the steamboat backed away and swung into midstream; he was really going at last. He crept from beneath the boat and sat looking out over the water and enjoying the scenery. Then it began to rain—a terrific downpour. He crept back under the boat, but his legs were outside, and one of the crew saw him. So he was taken down into the cabin and at the next stop set ashore. It was the town of Louisiana [Missouri], and there were Lampton [his mother's family] relatives there who took him home. Jane Clemens declared that his father had got to take him in hand; which he did, doubtless impressing the adventure on him in the usual way [a lecture]."

Steamboats on the Mississippi River intrigued young Sam.

Once during their years in Hannibal the family was offered $250 for the land, far less than what it was worth. As usual, they needed money, so even this offer was considered. Sam's brother Orion described it this way:

> If we had received that two hundred and fifty dollars, it would have been more than we ever made, clear of expenses, out of the whole of the Tennessee land, after forty years of worry to three generations.[6]

Hannibal as Inspiration

Living in a bigger city and observing his father's law practice exposed young Sam to crime—even murder. Once Sam saw a slave killed just because his owner did not like the way the slave completed a task. He saw a murder committed only a few yards from his house on Hill Street, while another time he saw a widow use a musket to kill a rowdy stranger who threatened her. One night when he was eight Sam discovered the body of a murdered man in his father's office. These unusual experiences all became fodder for later books. For example, the stranger killed by the widow became part of Injun Joe's revenge in *Tom Sawyer*. The drunks, murderers, and people who mistreated black people in *Huckleberry Finn* were also townspeople from Hannibal.

The murder of the slave that Sam witnessed was just one example of an attitude that prevailed throughout the town of Hannibal. Hannibal was essentially a Southern town in manner and disposition, which meant that most people were prejudiced against blacks. Local superstition told children to be afraid of black people.

Mark Twain revisits his home in Hannibal, Missouri, where his childhood adventures provided the material for many stories in Tom Sawyer *and* Huckleberry Finn.

Runaway slaves were generally considered to be as dangerous as wild beasts and were to be treated accordingly.

Sam saw prejudice displayed in his own household as well. Although the Clemens family was relatively poor, they managed to hire two black servants: Jennie, a servant who came with the family from Florida, and Uncle Ned, a handyman who helped around the house. When Jennie talked back, Mrs. Clemens called her high-spirited and a source of trouble. Sam began to question the rightness of slavery at a young age, though he dared not do so publicly. It is no accident that Jim in *Huckleberry Finn* is represented as a thinking, caring human being who simply wants to lead a life of freedom. When *Huckleberry Finn* was written, no author had ever treated black and white characters as equals in a novel, as Twain did with Jim and Huck Finn.

Boyhood Adventures

Despite the darker elements of life in Hannibal, Sam found plenty of friends and lots of places to have fun. Over the years they explored every corner of Hannibal and the surrounding area. All of the places made famous in *The Adventures of Tom Sawyer* and *The Adventures of Huckleberry Finn* were based on Hannibal. For example, Tom Sawyer and Becky Thatcher's experience in "McDougal's Cave," is based on a real Hannibal location, Dr. McDowell's limestone cave. The steamboats, the rafts, the island in the river where Huck and Tom and Jim hide out are all real, and we can rest assured that young Sam Clemens and his childhood buddies explored them all.

Most colorful of all Sam's playmates was his best friend, Tom Blankenship. Tom had freedoms few boys enjoyed: he came and went from home as he pleased and spent the majority of his time on the river, fishing and hunting. Tom even claimed to know spells and incantations. Compared to other boys he was like a wild thing and the most exciting companion a boy could have. Twain immortalized Tom as Huck Finn. In fact, Huck's house, as described in the novel, is a vivid depiction of Tom's boyhood home.

The real-life adventures of Sam and Tom and their friends John Briggs and Will Bowen provide the basis for many stories in *Tom Sawyer* and *Huckleberry Finn*. In fact, the relationship of Huck Finn and Jim was inspired by a real-life incident.

An Uncle Ned Story

Albert Bigelow Paine, a Twain biographer, presents a typical Uncle Ned story:

"Once 'pon a time there was a man, and he was riding along de road and he come to a ha'nted [haunted] house, and he heard chains a-rattlin' and a-rattlin' and a-rattlin', and a ball of fire come rollin' up and got under his stirrup, and it didn't make no difference if his horse galloped or went slow or stood still, de ball of fire staid [stayed] under his stirrup till he got plum to de front do' [door], and his wife come out and say: 'My Gord [God], dat's devil fire!' and she had to work a witch spell to drive it away.

At this point, one or several of the Clemens children would shout: 'How big was it, Uncle Ned?'

'Oh, 'bout as big as your head, and I 'spect [suspect] it's likely to come down dis yere [this here] chimney 'most any time!'"

(Below) Many slaves risked harsh punishment and even death trying to escape the bonds of slavery. Twain, who questioned the rightness of slavery, allowed Jim to experience a happier fate in Huckleberry Finn (left).

Ben Blankenship, Tom's older brother, discovered a runaway slave from Monroe County, Missouri, hiding outside Hannibal. Instead of turning the man in for the fifty dollar reward that the poor boy could definitely have used, Ben fed the man all summer. Finally some woodchoppers discovered the slave's hideout and chased him through a marsh, where the unfortunate fugitive drowned. In *Huckleberry Finn*, however, Mark Twain allows Jim to experience a happier fate when Huck Finn and Tom Sawyer help Jim escape his captors.

Sam Gets Some Schooling

Like Tom Sawyer, Sam Clemens hated school. Sam attended three different one-room schoolhouses while his father was alive, quitting eventually at the age of thirteen. His education began at the age of four and a half in a makeshift school run by Mrs. Elizabeth Horr, the wife of Hannibal's cooper (barrel maker). For twenty-five cents a week she taught a dozen or so students of varying ages prayers, the Bible, and McGuffey's Readers (nineteenth-century basic education books). Then came study with an Irishman named Cross, and study with J.D. Dawson in 1847 when Sam was twelve. Dawson was the model for Mr. Dobbins in *Tom Sawyer*, and probably just as boring to young Sam.

Although school work was not a priority for him, young Sam excelled at spelling. In Cross's and Dawson's classes, he regularly received the medal given for winning the spelling bees that were usually held once a week.

Death and Lost Hopes

As Sam struggled with school, his family struggled with personal finances and tragedy. Despite all his jobs, John Clemens failed to prosper in Hannibal. His resolve to improve things was shaken in 1842, when young Benjamin "took sick" and died (the actual cause of death is unknown). Another major disappointment came when Sam's older brother Orion was forced to leave his father's employ at the family store in Hannibal and become a printer's apprentice for the Hannibal *Journal* newspaper. The family felt that Orion's pursuit of a trade was a social step downward and only made the family's woes seem more severe.

In 1847, after going bankrupt, John Clemens died of pneumonia at the age of forty-nine. Everyone in the family now had to contribute to the group's survival. For twelve-year-old Sam, that meant working as a printer's "devil" or apprentice alongside his brother at the *Journal* after

school. This was the beginning of a ten-year career in newspapers that would include being a full-time apprentice, Orion's assistant editor, and a journeyman printer around the country.

A Writer Is Born

As Sam learned the printer's trade at the *Journal*, he began writing stories. He wrote about what he knew best—Hannibal. Sam had committed to memory every detail about Hannibal, good and bad, so writing stories about the town was relatively easy. In 1851 he succeeded in publishing two short nonfiction stories about Hannibal in Philadelphia's *Saturday Evening Post*. A year later at the age of sixteen, under the signature "S.L.C." Boston's humor magazine *The Carpet-Bag* published "The Yankee Frightening the Squatter." In the same month, May 1852, he again wrote about Hannibal for the *American Courier* in Philadelphia, but this time he wrote something purely imaginary about Indians who had once visited Hannibal:

> But where now are the children of the forest? Hushed is the war-cry—no more does the light canoe cut the crystal waters of the Mississippi; but the remnant of those once powerful tribes are torn asunder and scattered abroad, and now they wander far, far from the homes of their childhood and the graves of their fathers.[7]

Unfortunately, Sam was not paid for any of the stories. Still, these early publications allowed him to dream of greater success and fueled his desire to wander far from the home of his childhood. It was

An Excerpt from *Tom Sawyer, Detective*

Mark Twain wrote three books about the character Tom Sawyer. In the last one Tom and Huckleberry Finn solve a murder case. Tom's testimony to the jury reveals Twain's mastery of the character, who sounds just like a young boy:

"There was a steamboat laying at Flagler's Landing, forty miles above here, and it was raining and storming like the nation. And there was a thief aboard, and he had them two big di'monds that's advertised out here on this court-house door; and he slipped ashore with his hand-bag and struck out into the dark and the storm, and he was a-hoping he could get to this town all right and be safe. But he had two pals aboard the boat, hiding, and he knowed they was going to kill him the first chance they got and take the di'monds; because all three stole them, and then this fellow he got hold of them and skipped.

Well, he hadn't been gone more'n ten minutes before his pals found it out, and they jumped ashore and lit out after him. Prob'ly they burnt matches and found his tracks. Anyway, they dogged along after him all day Saturday and kept out of his sight; and towards sundown he come to the bunch of sycamores down by Uncle Silas' field, and he went in there to get a disguise out of his hand-bag and put it on before he showed himself here in the town—and mind you he done that just a little after the time that Uncle Silas was hitting Jubiter Dunlap over the head with a club—for he *did* hit him."

one thing to dream of the world, however, and quite another to really go out into it. Yet leave he did. In June 1853 he departed from Hannibal, but only after swearing on the Bible to his mother that he would keep away from cards and drinking. Sam's first destination was St. Louis, not all that far from Hannibal. Luckily for generations of readers to come, he had other destinations in mind, and other adventures, too.

2 Life on the Mississippi

Eighteen-year-old Sam, already trained as a printer and editor at the Hannibal newspaper, set out to make a living as a typesetter. His first stop was St. Louis, where his sister Pamela had moved after marrying a well-to-do merchant named William A. Moffett. Sam got a job in the composing room of the St. Louis *Evening News*, staying only long enough to earn enough money to reach New York City, where the Crystal Palace World's Fair was in progress. In a letter to Pamela we see the beginnings of Clemens's descriptive powers:

> From the gallery [second floor] you have a glorious sight—the flags of the different countries represented, the lofty dome, glittering jewelry, gaudy tapestry, etc., with the busy crowd passing to and fro—'tis a perfect fairy palace—beautiful beyond description. . . . The visitors to the Palace average 6,000 daily—double the population of Hannibal. The price of admission being 50 cents, they take in about $3,000.[8]

Sam had arrived in New York with a few dollars in his pocket and a ten-dollar bill sewn inside the lining of his coat. He got a job at a printing establishment for four dollars a week, and room and board

After a short stay in St. Louis, a restless Sam headed to New York City to see the glorious sights of the Crystal Palace World's Fair.

at a house on Duane Street. After expenses he was able to save about fifty cents a week.

He stayed only a few months in New York. Anxious to see the world, he soon moved to Philadelphia and got a job at the *Inquirer*, a daily newspaper. He was convinced he could survive anywhere, and he liked Philadelphia much more than New York. He was fascinated by the city, which was much larger than Hannibal, and its historical sites, including the graves of Benjamin and Deborah Franklin, were of great interest to Sam. Franklin's life greatly impressed Sam, and it is interesting that their lives seemed similar. As Albert Bigelow Paine put it:

> Each learned the printer's trade; each worked in his brother's printing office and wrote for the paper; each left quietly and went to New York, and from New York to Philadelphia, as a journeyman printer; each in due season became a world figure, many-sided, human, and of incredible popularity.[9]

Although Sam submitted a few poems to the Philadelphia *Ledger*, which were turned down, he generally forgot about writing until Orion, who had bought a newspaper office in Muscatine, Iowa, urged Sam to contribute. A letter to Orion explained Sam's temporary abandonment of writing:

> I will try to write for [Orion's] paper occasionally, but I fear my letters will be very uninteresting, for this incessant night work dulls one's ideas amazingly. . . . I believe I am the only person in the *Inquirer* office that does not drink. One young fellow makes $18 for a few weeks [of work], and gets on

Orion Clemens, who owned his own newspaper office in Iowa, urged his younger brother Sam to contribute his writings to the paper.

a grand "bender" [drunk] and spends every cent of it.[10]

Working as a typesetter was hard, demanding work that required great attention to detail, and Sam found little enjoyment in it. He did not start drinking to forget his woes as some of his friends did, but he was too mentally drained by his job to do much more than see the sights in his free hours.

Sam began to grow restless and homesick. In January 1854 he quit his typesetting job and made a short trip to Washington, D.C., went back to Philadelphia to

Sam's career as a typesetter was shortlived; he found the job demanding and quickly tired of it.

briefly work for two papers, then returned to New York. By late summer he could stand being away from home no longer. He took a train to Muscatine, where Orion and most of the Clemens family were living.

Orion wanted Sam to work for him. Having experienced Orion's financial ups and downs before, however, Sam declined. Instead, he went to St. Louis to work on the *Evening News*. Orion married on the spur of the moment and moved to Keokuk, Iowa. Between the summer and winter of 1855, Sam visited Orion, and his brother offered Sam five dollars a week and room and board to work as a journeyman printer. This time Sam accepted the job and worked for his brother for most of two years.

Dreams of Adventure

Working with his brother did not quiet Sam's desire for adventure, however. While in Keokuk Sam read Lieutenant Herndon's description of his survey of the upper Amazon River, including tales of natives who could stay awake for days by eating coca leaves (cocaine is derived from coca leaves). Sam did not take the drug— he only read about it. Although it sounds terrible (considering what we know today about the drug), Sam dreamed of becoming rich by harvesting coca for North American distribution. At the time coca was considered an herb with magical properties. To achieve his goal of becoming rich off cocaine, Sam had to raise the money for a trip to South America. As if guided by a divine hand, a solution came floating on the wind. In early November 1857, Sam was walking down Main Street in Keokuk when he grabbed a bit of paper as it flew past him. It was a fifty-dollar bill. He had no idea where this startling find had flown from. In an article called "The Turning Point of My Life," written many years later, he said "I advertised the find and left for the Amazon the same day."[11]

The statement is not exactly true—he stayed around longer than that—but it was still quite a stroke of luck. No one claimed the money, though Sam admitted he didn't describe it very specifically. He decided that this was truly a sign that he should pursue his South American journey as soon as possible. He first visited his mother, who now lived in St. Louis. While there, he got an idea to make more money from his adventures when he returned to Keokuk and made a deal with George Rees at a Keokuk newspaper, the *Saturday Post*. Rees agreed to buy Sam's descriptions of his South American journey for five dollars a letter, a good sum in those days.

Sam Clemens, Cub Pilot

Sam sold only two letters that described his proposed journey before taking a job at a Cincinnati printing office. By the spring of 1857 Sam was twenty-one and had saved enough money to go to South America. He boarded the steamer *Paul Jones* at Cincinnati, Ohio, which would take him to New Orleans, where he could board the ship that would take him to South America. While on the way to Louisiana, Sam had time to think. Instead of resolving to continue with his dream of becoming a coca baron, he decided to pursue his boyhood ambition of becoming a master river pilot. Once again, luck was with him.

Sam approached Horace Bixby, the pilot of the *Paul Jones*, in the pilothouse one morning, and told him of his desire to become a steamboat pilot. It turned out that Bixby and Sam had friends in common— the Bowen brothers, William, Sam, and Bart—now all river pilots. William, in fact, had done his first steering under Bixby.

Bixby liked Sam's slow drawl and easy manner, and Sam's honest reply to the pilot's questions amused him. The two hit it off, and, because Bixby had a sore foot that day, he let Sam take the wheel. After a while he offered a deal: he would take Sam on as a "cub," or learner, if Sam would pay him five hundred dollars. Sam countered with an offer of one hundred dollars cash and the rest when he earned it. Bixby agreed. He began teaching Sam immediately, which gave him a chance to nurse his sore foot.

When they reached New Orleans, Sam discovered that no boats were leaving for South America any time soon. He considered this a sign that fate had intervened in

Horace Bixby, the pilot of the Paul Jones, *agreed to take Clemens on as an apprentice. Under Bixby's tutelage, Sam fulfilled his childhood dream of becoming a master steamboat pilot.*

Calling "Mark Twain"

River depth was measured with a cord weighted with lead by the leadsmen, who stayed at the front of the steamboat and called out what they found. It was a crucial process that often meant the difference between safe passage and wrecking the boat. The leadsmen's cries were echoed along the boat by other deckhands, until word reached the pilot. A "mark" was a fathom (six feet), so "mark twain" meant the water was twelve feet deep. Twain describes the process in Life on the Mississippi:

"The cries of the leadsmen began to rise out of the distance, and were gruffly repeated by the word-passers on the hurricane-deck [top deck].

'M-a-r-k three! M-a-r-k three! Quarter less three! Half twain! Quarter twain! M-a-r-k twain! Quarter-less—'

Mr. Bixby pulled two bell-ropes, and was answered by faint jinglings far below in the engine-room, and our speed slackened. The steam began to whistle through the gaugecocks. The cries of the leadsmen went on—and it is a weird sound, always, in the night. Every pilot in the lot was watching now, with fixed eyes, and talking under his breath. Nobody was calm and easy but Mr. Bixby. He would put his wheel down and stand on a spoke [of the wheel], and as the steamer swung into her (to me) utterly invisible marks—for we seemed to be in the midst of a wide and gloomy sea—he would meet and fasten her there. Out of the murmur of half-audible talk, one caught a coherent sentence now and then—such as:

'There; she's over the first reef all right!'

After a pause, another subdued voice:

'Her stern's coming down just *exactly* right, by George!'

Somebody else muttered:

'Oh, it was done beautiful—*beautiful!*' "

his destiny. He went back to St. Louis on the steamboat, borrowed enough money from his brother-in-law, William Moffett, to complete his first payment to Bixby, then returned to New Orleans.

Sam had originally "supposed all that a pilot had to do was to keep his boat in the river."[12] He quickly found out how difficult the job could be. Bixby impressed upon his cub that navigating the twelve hundred miles of rapidly shifting water that made up the Mississippi could be treacherous. He instructed Sam to get a notebook and take notes every time he gave him an instruction. Sam later recalled this training as enhancing his already sharp memory. In *Life on the Mississippi* he reflected:

I think a pilot's memory is about the most wonderful thing in the world. . . . Give a man a tolerably fair memory to start with, and piloting will develop it into a very colossus [giant] of capability. . . . Astonishing things can be done with the human memory if you will devote it faithfully to one particular line of business.[13]

The Strange Death of Henry Clemens

While Sam learned his craft quickly, he experienced a severe emotional blow. In 1858 his brother Henry was killed while crewing on the steamboat *Pennsylvania* on which Sam also worked as a steersman. The pilot of the *Pennsylvania* was a tyrannical, foul-mouthed man named Brown. One day while they were all three in the pilothouse, Brown hit Henry after Brown himself had been chewed out by the captain for not acting on an order that Henry had relayed. In defense of his brother, Sam knocked Brown down and beat him up. Because Sam worked under Brown, this was a serious offense and could have resulted in Sam's being fired. But the captain also hated Brown and arranged for Sam to follow on another boat back to St. Louis, where he would take over Brown's pilot job.

The *Pennsylvania* never made it to St. Louis. Four of its eight boilers blew up near Memphis, and over 150 people died. Henry was thrown free, relatively uninjured. He chose to swim back, however, to try to save others. Unfortunately, he died in a Memphis hospital from injuries incurred in the rescue attempt.

When Sam came for the body, he discovered that the ladies of Memphis—who had tried to nurse the young, handsome Henry back to health—had made up a fund and bought a metallic liner for Henry's wooden coffin. When Sam entered the room, he saw Henry in the coffin, with white flowers on his chest. A woman entered the room and placed a single red rose directly in the middle of the other flowers. Sam experienced a terrible sense of déjà vu. Months before, Sam had had a vivid dream in which he pictured this exact scene. Sam's awful dream was complete; the incident renewed his lifelong interest in the supernatural.

Sam Clemens, River Pilot

Sam managed to press on in spite of the loss and was granted his pilot's license on April 9, 1859. Fellow river pilot and friend Horace Bixby told an interviewer years later that Sam passed the apprenticeship in only eighteen months. Other accounts say it took two years. Either way, it was a relatively short period of time, considering the intricacies of the Mississippi and the enormous amount of detail a pilot had to remember. Soon Sam was making nearly $250 a month, as much as a justice of the Supreme Court, or the vice president of the United States. Even better, he did not have to pay for lodging or food while he was on the river. He was able to send money home to his mother and even to loan some to Orion.

Because of the thousands of twists and turns of the Mississippi, with underwater shoals and wrecked boats to be wary of, all pilots kept a log book. The river was constantly changing, so new notations had to be made all the time. Sam, however, used his notebooks for more than just river notations. In one he wrote out an exercise in

Steamboats round the bend of the scenic Mississippi River. Clemens quickly learned the intricacies of the river and became a skilled pilot.

French, from the writings of French philosopher Voltaire. Another notation prophesied Clemens's future:

> How to Take Life.—Take it just as though it was—as it is—an earnest, vital and important affair. Take it as though you were born to the task of performing a merry part in it—as though the world had awaited . . . your coming. Take it as though it was a grand opportunity to do and achieve, to carry forward great and good schemes; to help and cheer a suffering, weary, it may be heartbroken, brother. Now and then a man stands aside from the crowd, labors earnestly, steadfastly, confidently, and straight-away becomes famous for wisdom, intellect, skill, greatness of some sort. The world wonders, admires, idolizes, and it only illustrates what others may do if they take hold of life with a purpose. The miracle, or the power that elevates the few, is to be found in their industry, application, and perseverance under the promptings of a brave, determined spirit.[14]

Sam Goes After Mark Twain

Sam was popular as a pilot, regarded as safe, and as such was given large and difficult boats. He gathered quite a reputation

Knowing the River like a Book

To get some idea of what a river pilot looked for on the river, consider this excerpt from Twain's Life on the Mississippi:

"The face of the water, in time, became a wonderful book—a book that was a dead language to the uneducated passenger, but which told its mind to me without reserve, delivering its most cherished secrets as clearly as if it uttered them with a voice. And it was not a book to be read once and thrown aside, for it had a new story to tell every day. Throughout the long twelve hundred miles there was never a page that was void of interest, never one that you could leave unread without loss, never one that you wanted to skip, thinking you could find higher enjoyment in some other thing. There never was so wonderful a book written by man; never one whose interest was so absorbing, so unflagging, so sparkingly renewed with each reperusal. The passenger who could not read it was charmed with a peculiar sort of faint dimple on its surface (on the rare occasions when he did not overlook it altogether); but to the pilot that was an *italicized* passage; indeed, it was more than that, it was a legend of the largest capitals, with a string of shouting exclamation points at the end of it, for it meant that a wreck or a rock was buried there that could tear the life out of the strongest vessel that ever floated. It is the faintest and simplest expression the water ever makes, and the most hideous to a pilot's eye."

Twain compared the Mississippi River to a book that had a "new story to tell every day."

as a storyteller, too. Horace Bixby remembered that "Sam was always scribbling when not at the wheel."[15] The only memorable thing Sam published during his piloting days, though, was a satire of an old pilot named Isaiah Sellers who regularly contributed to the New Orleans *Picayune* under the name Mark Twain. Sellers was known to exaggerate his abilities as a pilot and his length of service. The young pilots loved to mock his stories. Sam signed his satirical piece of fiction Sergeant Fathom. His fellow pilot Bart Bowen loved it and got it printed in the paper *True Delta* in May 1859.

The piece was widely read and enjoyed. Its mockery of Mark Twain was so easily recognizable and so humiliating that Sellers never wrote another paragraph for the *Picayune*. Sam felt badly about the effect his story had on Sellers. When he later took up the name Mark Twain himself, it was partly in deference to the old man he had thoughtlessly wounded.

Visit with a Psychic

Once Sam had mastered piloting, his life entered a somewhat carefree period. He made enough money to afford extravagant ten-dollar dinners. He took his mother, his cousin Ella Creel, and another young woman on a tour of New Orleans. Still, despite the prospect of being set for life, Sam was uncertain of his future. Henry's death had shown him that a promising young life could end unexpectedly. Thus, early in 1861 he visited a famous New Orleans psychic known as Madame Capprell. He then reported to Orion in a letter dated February 6 that the

The Slowest Boat on the River

Sam loved steamboat races. He describes the contests in great detail in Life on the Mississippi. *One of the boats he piloted was a large, slow boat that he said was good only in races with "islands, and rafts and such things":*

"There is a great difference in boats. For a long time I was on a boat that was so slow we used to forget what year it was we left port in. But of course this was at rare intervals. Ferry-boats used to lose valuable trips because their passengers grew old and died, waiting for us to get by. This was at still rarer intervals. I had the documents for these occurrences, but through carelessness they have been mislaid. This boat, the *John J. Roe*, was so slow that when she finally sunk in Madrid Bend it was five years before the owners heard of it. This was always a confusing fact to me, but it is according to the record, anyway. She was dismally slow; still, we often had pretty exciting times racing with islands, rafts, and such things."

The outbreak of the Civil War made travel on the Mississippi River dangerous and forced Clemens to quit his job as a river pilot.

clairvoyant told Sam that Orion should devote himself to his business and to politics with all his might and that Orion could hold government office. She told Sam that a turning point in his life occurred in "1840-7-3, which was it?" (His father had died in 1847.) Then she said the following:

> You might have distinguished yourself as an orator, or as an editor; you have written a great deal; you write well—but you are rather out of practice; no matter—you will be *in* practice some day.[16]

Sam had no way of knowing how right she would be. In the letter to Orion he wrote that he was "under the decided impression that going to the fortune-teller's was just as good as going to the opera, and cost a trifle more."[17] In other words, it was merely entertainment.

The clairvoyant was wrong about one major item. She predicted that Sam would retire from piloting in ten years. Instead, his career ended only two months later, with the outbreak of the Civil War. The river pilots were as divided on the issue of North versus South as anyone in the United States. Traffic on the Mississippi and other major rivers could no longer flow freely—it was now tightly controlled by military forces of both sides. Horace Bixby took the Union side and became chief of the Union River Service. When Bixby made that choice, Sam felt he had to quit. There was always the possibility he would be forced to pilot a Union gunboat, and Sam loved the South too much to let that happen. Not ready to join either the Confederacy or the Union immediately, he boarded a steamer named *Uncle Sam* and decided to go home and think it over. The *Uncle Sam* was fired upon by Union troops in St. Louis, then examined by Union forces and passed. It was the last steamboat to make the trip from New Orleans on a commercial journey until after the Civil War, and Sam Clemens was certain his piloting days were over. Now, whether he liked it or not, he would have to pick sides in a war that he didn't really believe in.

Chapter
3 Roughing It

When the Civil War broke out in 1861, Sam Clemens, like millions of other Americans at the time, was simply trying to make up his mind about which side, North or South, he would support. Sam's decision was complicated by the fact that he came from Missouri, a border state, caught in the middle between Northern free states and Southern slave states. Slavery was not practiced in the industrialized Northern states like New York or Massachusetts. In Southern states like Virginia, however, where the economy was mostly based on agriculture, many people used slaves as cheap labor. Southerners believed that paying field hands to tend and harvest such crops as cotton would make it economically impossible for plantations to make a profit.

The United States might have simply remained split over these issues without coming to war, except for one thing—whether new states, as they were admitted to the Union, should allow the practice of slavery. Whether a new state chose to be a slave or free state would upset the overall balance of the States, and each side was afraid that the other would gain too much political power.

Men from Missouri joined both sides

Southern plantations relied heavily on cheap slave labor. Thus, many Southerners feared that the abolition of slavery would cripple their economy.

Confederate general Robert E. Lee surveys a battle-ground during the Civil War. Like Lee, Clemens chose to join the Confederate side despite his dislike of slavery.

of the conflict, but Hannibal's Southern attitudes made the majority pro-slavery. When Sam arrived in his hometown, he encountered a "defend our home" attitude. Like Confederate general Robert E. Lee, Sam Clemens loved the United States but felt he had to defend his home state from invading Union forces. Lee, a high-ranking U.S. Army general before the war, had been offered the command of the Union forces. Loyal to his home state of Virginia, Lee instead chose to lead the Army of the Confederacy, even though he did not have slaves himself and did not believe in slavery.

Sam made up his mind: despite his own dislike for the practice of slavery, he considered the Union troops to be invaders that must be repelled. Sam joined with a group of old schoolmates and out-of-work river pilots like himself—Sam Bowen, Ed Stevens, and Ab Grimes—and formed a battalion to fight for the South. They said goodbye to family and friends, and marched through the night to New London, Missouri, to be sworn in as Confederate troops.

The next morning a Colonel Ralls of Ralls County swore the men into Confederate service. Ralls sent out word to his neighbors such as Colonel Bill Splawn and farmer Nuck Matson, and donations began arriving from the community to support the new battalion. Sam ended up with a yellow mule named Paint Brush to ride. He soon developed a boil [skin inflammation] to add to his woes, and found soldiering not much to his liking.

The men marched and camped, looking for Union troops to fight. When they camped near Sam's birthplace of Florida, Missouri, one man acted as barber, cutting the men's long hair with sheep shears. The reasoning was that, should they get into hand-to-hand fights with the enemy, no one could grab their hair and get an advantage. They elected officers. Sam became a second lieutenant, but it meant nothing; almost everyone in the outfit was an officer.

When it began raining, day and night, the little band found itself slogging through mud with no enemy in sight. After about three weeks the men were a pretty ragged bunch. Other than firing some shots in the dark during false alarms, the "Marion Rangers," as they called themselves, were at war only in their minds. Hungry, tired and disillusioned, they camped out one night in Colonel Bill Splawn's barn. After Sam went to sleep one of the soldiers lit up a

The Overland Barns in Carson City, Nevada, served as a post for traveling stages. Sam and Orion probably made the journey to Carson City in a stagecoach much like the one seen in this picture.

smoke, and set the hay on fire. Someone yelled "Fire!" Sam woke up, jumped out of the second-floor window, and sprained his ankle. The other soldiers, not knowing he had jumped, began searching for him under the hay, and in the process started to toss burning hay on top of him! Sam forgot his injured ankle and scurried to safety. He wrote later that he didn't stop cursing until he covered both sides of the Civil War and humanity in general.

The next morning, after breakfast, the injured Sam was deposited at Nuck Matson's farm. As soon as he was able to travel, he said goodbye to the Confederacy and war, and left for Keokuk, Iowa, where Orion was going. Sam later wrote about his short time in the war—with some fictional and antiwar changes—in the story, "Private History of a Campaign That Failed."

Go West, Young Sam

Sam discovered that Orion had just been appointed secretary of the Nevada territory by his old friend Edward Bates, who was a member of President Lincoln's cabinet. As secretary, Orion would act as governor in the governor's absence and perform other duties.

Orion had to get to Nevada to assume the post, but he had no money. So Sam made a deal with him. If Orion would make him his personal secretary, Sam would supply the money for both of them to go West. Orion agreed. Sam had the job but would receive no salary. They immediately set out for St. Joseph, Missouri, where they would catch the Overland Mail Company's stage. On July 26, 1861, they left on a nineteen-day, seventeen-hundred-mile trip to Carson City, Nevada. Sam loved the journey almost as much as riding on a riverboat. He wrote about it years later in *Roughing It:*

> Even at this day it thrills me through and through to think of the life, the gladness, and the wild sense of freedom that used to make the blood dance in my face on those fine Overland mornings.[18]

On August 14 Sam and Orion reached Carson City, capital of the Nevada Territory, and were received by Governor Nye and a committee. When the officials saw the dusty, grimy, weather-beaten Clemens brothers, the reception quickly dispersed. Sam and Orion had not made a very good first impression.

Orion set about changing that image, and his industriousness made an immediately favorable impression on the people of Carson City. Sam was another story. Orion had little need for a secretary, so there was nothing for Sam to do. People openly commented on how lazy he seemed to be.

Since he still had money saved up, Sam was in no hurry to jump into the only other profession available in Nevada: the mining business. Realizing that his public image reflected disfavorably on Orion, Sam decided to move on since he had found something that he thought would make money: timber. There were thousands of acres of virgin western forest just waiting to be harvested and sold, Sam reasoned. Together with a new friend from Ohio named John Kinney, he visited Lake Bigler (now named Lake Tahoe), to stake out a claim. Sam fell in love with the area, but a camping accident set thousands of acres of woods on fire, so he and Kinney came back to Carson City.

Getting the Gold Bug

In early winter Sam finally caught mining fever. In fact he became consumed by it. All his letters home were filled with descriptions of mining terms and future fortunes. It was not hard to understand why—cartloads of silver and gold bricks were driven daily through the streets of Carson City. Sam set out north with a blacksmith and two young lawyer friends, Gus Oliver and W.H. Clagget, to Humboldt County, where it was reported that the mountains were literally bursting with gold and silver.

Because a war with the Indians had recently occurred in the area they were passing through, the party occasionally saw burned-down shacks and fresh graves. Then came the barren Alkali Desert, and they traveled all day and night to cross it. It was three o'clock in the morning before

Miners report for work in a Nevada silver mine. News of gold and silver strikes enticed thousands of prospectors, including Clemens and several of his friends, to the West.

and then with his inimitable drawl said: "Boys, they have left us our scalps. Let's give them all the flour and sugar they ask for." And we did give them a good supply, for we were grateful.[19]

The mining expedition was as great a failure as Sam's quest for harvestable timber. Sam never found an ounce of gold, only sparkling but worthless mica. Less than two months later the men were back in Carson City, their expedition a bust.

Saved by the Pen

When Sam returned, he found that Orion was having trouble with the governor. Orion was a stickler for keeping accurate books; his integrity regarding financial dealings was above question. The governor treated the accounting of government money quite differently, spending as he pleased. When he and Orion clashed over this, Sam took it upon himself to have a talk with the governor behind closed doors. Whatever he said did the trick. The governor was much easier on Orion and developed quite a friendship with Sam.

Still, the brothers' finances were in bad shape. Sam tried mining again, this time with the Esmeralda mines, in which he and Orion both held stock. In February 1862 he went to Aurora, on the California border, found a cabin with some other hopeful miners, and set about trying once again to find a fortune. By spring Sam had learned quite a bit about digging and blasting and still felt he would be rich any day. By summer, however, he had quit mining and went to work as a common laborer in a quartz mill at ten dollars a

Clemens's cabin in Aurora, California, where, despite previous failure, he set out to make his fortune in mining.

they made camp. They were awakened the next day by a war party of Paiute Indians. According to Gus Oliver, Sam Clemens made a deal with the Indians:

The sun was high in the heavens when we were aroused from our sleep by a yelling band of [Paiute] warriors. We were upon our feet in an instant. The pictures of burning cabins and the lonely graves we had passed were in our minds. Our scalps were still our own, and not dangling from the belts of our visitors. Sam pulled himself together, put his hand on his head as if to make sure he had not been scalped, week. One biographer later suggested that Sam took the job only to learn the art of refining, but Twain said in *Roughing It* that he was broke. Whatever the truth, Sam's prospects for the future looked dismal.

It was writing that saved him from the drudgery of labor. His mother had given some of Sam's letters describing his adventures to the editor of the Keokuk, Iowa, newspaper *Gate City*, and the editor published them. When Orion received copies of the newspaper, he showed them to a man named Barstow from the Nevada *Territorial Enterprise.* Sam was contacted by the *Enterprise* and sent in letters that he signed Josh. (He did not want to use his real name, because he thought he would be-

A 1907 photograph of Steve Gillis, the printing foreman of the Nevada Territorial Enterprise. *Gillis and Twain hit it off immediately and became best friends.*

come a mining millionaire any day and people might come looking for him to borrow money.)

In July 1862 Barstow offered Sam twenty-five dollars a week to write for the newspaper full time. By August Sam was in Virginia City, ready to go to work. He was broke and disgusted with mining. At the paper he made an even worse first impression than when he and Orion had come off the Overland stage and met the governor. It is no wonder—he had walked the 130 miles from Aurora to Virginia City and had a beard halfway down his chest.

Joe Goodman, the paper's editor, was not pleased with his bearded visitor until Sam produced Barstow's letter inviting him to write for the paper. Goodman then welcomed him warmly and introduced him to the rest of the staff. The last introduction was to Steve Gillis, the printing foreman, whom Goodman instructed to help Sam get a haircut, shave and bath, new clothes, and a place to stay. Steve and Sam hit it off from the first and became best friends. William Gillis, Steve's brother, describes Sam's comments at that first meeting:

> Mr. Gillis, I don't often cotton [take a liking] to a man on first acquaintance, but I do cotton to you, right here and now, and I know we're going to be friends right from the start.[20]

Becoming Mark Twain

The *Enterprise* was the most popular newspaper in the West, and its style reflected the wild and wooly character of the Nevada Territory. Everyone who wrote for

Another Explanation for "Mark Twain"

This account from Ivan Benson's Mark Twain's Western Years *appeared in the* Nevada City *Transcript of February 22, 1866:*

"Sam . . . used to take his regular drinks at Johnny Doyle's . . . two horns [drinks] consecutive, one right after the other . . . on tick [credit]. . . . Johnny used to sing out to the barkeep . . . and kept the score, 'mark twain,' whereupon the barkeep would score two drinks to Sam's account—and so it was, d'ye [do you] see, that he come to be called 'Mark Twain.'"

the *Enterprise* was given a fairly free hand editorially. Nothing could have pleased Sam Clemens more and he blossomed under these conditions. Some of his stories were factual, but he soon leaned toward complete—and controversial—fiction.

While Nevada residents easily saw the obvious exaggerations or humorous lies in Sam's *Enterprise* pieces, everything in the paper was accepted literally by those outside the territory. For example, Sam wrote a sketch about "The Petrified Man" who had supposedly been discovered in Humboldt County. The story was written to poke fun at a fellow named Sewall, a coroner and justice of the peace who was slow in supplying news to the paper. A number of periodicals, including a medical journal in England, picked up the story and printed it as factual. The story did not make Sewall's life any easier, but it greatly boosted Sam's popularity at the *Enterprise*.

Before long Sam was sent to Carson City to cover the Nevada legislature, and he made fun of the representatives and government constantly. Soon his articles, written in the form of letters to the *Enterprise*, were being copied and quoted all along the West Coast. They were unsigned; Sam no longer liked the Josh pen name and was looking for another. Then in early 1863 the news came to him that Isaiah Sellers—the old river pilot—had

In 1863 Samuel Clemens officially adopted the pen name Mark Twain.

died. He told Joe Goodman about the name he wanted to use, and Joe agreed that it was a good one. Sam's first letter under the name Mark Twain appeared on February 2, 1863. Members of the legislature and some of his friends immediately began to address him as Mark instead of Sam. Clemens would forever be known to his readers as Mark Twain.

He became a celebrity while at the *Enterprise* and learned what it meant to be one. Everyone in affluent Virginia City seemed to recognize Mark Twain instantly. He was able to send his mother twenty dollars every couple of weeks, and he and Orion still figured they would become millionaires from the mining stocks they owned.

Late in 1863 the humorist Artemus Ward came to Virginia City, intending to stay a few days to deliver his lectures, then move on. When Ward met the staff of the *Enterprise*, however, he enjoyed them so much that he stayed for three weeks. Ward and Twain became good friends, and Ward urged him to try giving humorous lectures. He also counseled Twain to write for eastern audiences and sent a letter of introduction to the editor of the influential New York *Sunday Mercury*.

The Poison Pen's Result

Meanwhile, Twain continued being the leading resident celebrity of the Nevada Territory. The Civil War might as well have been happening on another planet. Unfortunately, his comments about some local Civil War efforts led to a dramatic fall from grace for the *Enterprise*'s favorite reporter.

In an editorial of May 1864 Twain

While in Virginia City delivering his lectures, humorist Artemus Ward met Twain and the two became good friends. Ward encouraged Twain to try giving humorous lectures.

made a rather tasteless joke about money raised by a Carson City ladies aid society. Twain claimed the piece had been written while he was drunk and that he hadn't intended to offend anyone. Twain later claimed that neither he nor the editor had meant for the article to be printed. According to Twain, the letter had been found on his desk late at night by the printing foreman and printed without approval.

The truth was that Joe Goodman had gone on vacation and left Twain as acting editor of the paper. And the printing foreman in question was Twain's friend Steve Gillis, so the argument was a weak one. More likely, drunk or not, Mark Twain let

Mark Twain's Reporting Style

This description of how Mark Twain put his Nevada newspaper stories together was given by Alfred Doten to Albert Bigelow Paine and published in Mark Twain, A Biography:

"My father and Mark Twain were once detailed to go over to Como [Nevada] and write up some new mines that had been discovered over there. My father was on the Gold Hill *News*. He and Mark had not met before, but became promptly acquainted, and were soon calling each other by their first names.

They went to a little hotel at Carson, agreeing to do their work together the next morning. When morning came they set out, and suddenly on a corner Mark stopped and turned to my father, saying:

'By gracious, Alf! Isn't that a brewery?'

'It is, Mark. Let's go in.'

They did so, and remained there all day, swapping yarns, sipping beer, and lunching, going back to the hotel that night.

The next morning precisely the same thing occurred. When they were on the same corner, Mark stopped as if he had never been there before, and said:

'Good gracious, Alf! Isn't that a brewery?'

'It is, Mark. Let's go in.'

So again they went in, and stayed all day.

That happened again the next morning, and the next. Then my father became uneasy. A letter had come from Gold Hill, asking him where his report of the mine was. They agreed that next morning they would really begin the story; that they would climb to the top of a hill that overlooked the mines, and write it from there.

But the next morning, as before, Mark was surprised to discover the brewery, and once more they went in. A few moments later, however, a man who knew all about the mines—a mining engineer connected with them— came in. He was a godsend. My father set down a valuable, informing story, while Mark got a lot of entertaining mining yarns out of him.

Next day Virginia City and Gold Hill were gaining information from my father's article, and entertainment from Mark's story of the mines."

In Twain's day, a duel could avenge an insult or decide an argument. A tasteless joke made by Twain in the Enterprise *almost resulted in a duel with James Laird, an owner of a competing newspaper.*

his freedom of expression at the newspaper go a little too far.

Twain was quickly attacked in print by James Laird, one of the owners of the Virginia City *Daily Union* newspaper. Laird said:

> [Twain] . . . had no gentlemanly sense of professional propriety, [and] conveyed in every word, and in every purpose of all his words, such a groveling disregard for truth, decency and courtesy as to seem to court the distinction only of being understood as a vulgar liar.[21]

There were a few more written exchanges, and soon Twain and Laird agreed to a duel with Colt revolvers. This terrified both men, but neither wanted to back down. On the morning of the duel the men were practicing shooting on either side of a hill. Steve Gillis, who was Twain's second, or assistant, borrowed Twain's pistol to teach him how to shoot. Gillis immediately shot the head off a wild bird called a mud hen. He handed the pistol back to Twain just as Laird and his second came

over the hill. Laird asked who killed the bird. Gillis said it was Twain, whom he swore was a deadly shot. Laird immediately backed out of the duel.

This might have been the end of it, but when they got back to town, Jerry Driscoll, the foreman of the Virginia City grand jury, told Twain and Gillis they had another problem. As Gillis told the story, Driscoll informed them that a new law had just passed in the legislature

> making a duel a penitentiary offense for both principal and second, [which] was to be strictly enforced, and unless we got out of town in a limited number of hours we would be the first examples to test the new law.[22]

Once again Sam Clemens—now known far and wide as Mark Twain—had grown affluent, then been forced to seek his fortune elsewhere. He had earlier spent some time in San Francisco, California, and enjoyed it. So in May 1864 Mark Twain and Steve Gillis left for San Francisco. It was certainly better than going to prison.

4 Travels to Enchanted Lands

While writing for the Virginia City *Territorial Enterprise*, Twain contributed short articles to a San Francisco newspaper called the *Daily Morning Call*. After being forced to leave Nevada, he went to work for the *Call* on a regular basis. Twain soon disliked the job, however, because it called for straight, unadorned news gathering, and many hours of it. Twain later called the job "fearful drudgery—soulless drudgery—and almost destitute of interest." At nine in the morning, he showed up at the police court, to make note of the arrests. The rest of the day he and other *Call* reporters "raked the town from end

to end." If there were no fires to report, he wrote, "we started some." The work continued into the evening:

> At night we visited the six theaters, one after the other, seven nights in the week. We remained in each of those places five minutes, got the merest passing glimpse of play and opera, and with that for a text we "wrote up" those plays and operas, as the phrase goes, torturing our souls every night in the effort to find something to say about those performances which we had not said a couple of hundred times before.[23]

In San Francisco Twain worked as a reporter for a newspaper called the Daily Morning Call. *He later called the job "soulless drudgery."*

Despite their many differences, Bret Harte became Twain's friend and literary mentor.

A Transformation Takes Place

Perhaps as a relief from the *Call* drudgery, Twain began socializing with the bohemians—writers and artists who had come to California from New York. The term *bohemian* referred to the gypsy ways and unconventional lives they led. The acknowledged leader of San Francisco's bohemians was writer Bret Harte, who made a living as the private secretary to the superintendent of the U.S. mint. The mint's offices were in the same building as the *Call*, and Harte and Twain soon became friends, in spite of the great difference in their appearances. Twain dressed in a rough western manner while Harte dressed like an English gentleman.

Harte's stories about California mining camps were published regularly on the

East Coast and in Joe Goodman's *Golden Era*, then the leading California literary journal. Twain did not always agree with Harte, but he was eager to learn all he could from the man. Harte had a literary reputation; Twain wanted one, and so Harte became Twain's literary mentor. Twain later described the value of Harte's advice:

> Bret Harte trimmed and trained and schooled me patiently until he changed me from an awkward utterer of coarse grotesqueness to a writer of paragraphs and chapters that have found a certain favor in the eyes of even some of the very decentest people in the land.[24]

The relationship was shaken by a woman: Ina Coolbrith—who eventually became California's first poet laureate. Both men were infatuated with Ina, but she seemed to favor Harte. This infuriated Twain, and when he let Harte know of his anger, it damaged their friendship. Rivaling each other for a woman's love was not enough to break the men apart in literary matters, however. When Harte and another columnist named Charles Henry Webb started their own literary publication, the *Californian*, Twain came aboard quickly. As he explained in a letter to his mother and sister in Hannibal:

> I quit the *Era*, long ago. It wasn't hightoned enough. The *Californian* circulates among the highest class of the community, and it is the best weekly literary paper in the United States.[25]

The *Californian* lasted four years, through numerous financial ups and downs, before folding. Its major contribution to American literature may have been to help transform Mark Twain from a writer who once had been called "the Wild Humorist of the Pacific Slope" into someone who took writing seriously.

Many times in his life, just when Twain thought he had achieved success, something occurred that changed everything. This developed into a recurring pattern throughout his life. In San Francisco a crisis arose over his activities as a reporter and the antics of Steve Gillis, his friend from Virginia City.

Twain Is Run Out of San Francisco

Because he wrote little of a serious nature about politics or local officials, in Nevada Twain had been celebrated by the legislature and been friendly with the representatives. As a reporter in San Francisco, however, he got off on a completely different start with government officials. One of his early articles in the *Call* criticized the coroner for not providing a list of deaths, as was customary. He also continually commented on the city's police corruption. This started when he saw some butchers set their dogs on "an unoffending Chinaman" while a policeman nearby just looked on and laughed. Another time, Twain found a policeman asleep on the beat and fanned the official with a large cabbage leaf until a large crowd gathered.

In San Francisco Twain wrote for any publication that wanted him—literary or otherwise—but continued contributing to the Virginia City *Enterprise*. When several Twain articles in the *Enterprise* exposed the corruption of the San Francisco police department, a lawsuit was filed against the

paper by Martin G. Burke, the San Francisco chief of police. The suit might not have caused Twain to leave town if another incident hadn't dovetailed with it to make trouble for Twain.

Shortly after the police lawsuit hit the courts, Steve Gillis, who worked at the *Call* as a compositor, broke up a brawl in a saloon owned by "Big Jim" Casey. Gillis's interference prompted Casey to lock the saloon door and challenge Gillis. Gillis hit Casey with an empty glass pitcher, and Casey went down. Two policemen broke down the door, found Casey on the floor, and immediately arrested Gillis for assault and battery.

Now the police had something else to use against Twain because it was common knowledge that Steve Gillis was Mark Twain's close friend. In fact, Twain raised the five hundred dollars to bail Gillis out of jail. The day after the brawl Gillis and Twain learned that Big Jim Casey was in the county hospital and might die. If Casey died, Steve Gillis might be tried for murder. If that occurred, the paper might think Twain was more trouble than he was worth and would no longer use his articles.

Out of Town and Out of Work

Fortunately, Steve's brother Jim was visiting San Francisco at the time and offered the men refuge in his cabin on Jackass Hill, in the Tuolumne district of the California gold country. So, on December 4, 1864, Steve Gillis jumped bail, and Mark Twain left town with him. Once again the writer from Missouri was unexpectedly out of a career. But like a cat with nine lives,

A pocket miner pans for gold in the river streams of California. Twain made an attempt at pocket mining with his friend Jim Gillis, whose campfire stories inspired Twain to write a number of fictional pieces.

Twain would again land on his feet and come across with a story that would make him world famous.

Jim Gillis was a pocket miner, that is, he panned for gold in the river streams of Stanislaus County, then traced the gold flakes upstream to find pockets of gold ore. Twain made an attempt at pocket mining with Jim, but did not like it much. Perhaps it reminded him of the earlier drudgery of working in the mines in Nevada. He did find something about living with Jim Gillis that inspired him, though. Jim told stories around the fire at night, usually about his friend Dick Stoker. The stories inspired Twain to write some fictional pieces. Many later Mark Twain stories—the tale of Dick Baker's cat, the Jaybird and the Acorn from *A Tramp Abroad*, and "Burning Shame"—originated with Jim Gillis.

It was a story heard *with* Jim Gillis, however, that would start Twain's international career. On New Year's night 1865 the two men were in Calaveras County. Twain saw an unusual sight—a lunar rainbow in a light, drizzling rain. Twain thought it was an omen of good fortune. Perhaps he was right. Later that month they returned to Calaveras County, to a town called Angel's Camp. They spent rainy days—when they couldn't mine—in the local tavern, listening to stories told by Ben Coon, a former Illinois River pilot. One Coon story was about a frog belonging to a fellow named Coleman, who trained it to jump a great distance. Coleman, claimed Coon, lost a bet with a competitor when his opponent secretly filled Coleman's frog with buckshot before the race.

Twain jotted down the details of the story in his notebook. Shortly after that he left the mountains. Several months had passed since leaving San Francisco. Big Jim Casey had not died, and the police had not come looking for either Steve Gillis or Twain. Twain moved to Stockton, where he took up residence in the Occidental Hotel. Now that he had a more permanent residence, he tracked down his mail and found letters waiting for him from his humorist friend, Artemus Ward.

Ward wanted him to contribute a sketch for a new book. Unfortunately, Twain got the letters three months late and figured it was impossible to get the piece of writing into the book in time.

Twain again began writing for the *Enterprise*, with no repercussions. He also wrote occasionally for the *Californian*, and before long he ended up back in San Francisco. About this time Artemus Ward visited Twain in San Francisco. Twain related the story of the jumping frog and Ward told him there was still time to get the story into Ward's new book.

When Carleton and Company, Ward's publisher, received Twain's story—"Jim

A caricature shows Twain riding the "jumping frog of Calaveras County." The story of the jumping frog sparked Twain's rise to celebrity status.

Smiley and His Jumping Frog"—Ward's book was ready for press and too far along to include the story. But publisher Carleton liked the story and didn't want it wasted, so he gave it to his friend Henry Clapp, the publisher of New York's *Saturday Press*. The *Press* published the story on November 18, 1865, and its impact on Twain's career was immediate. The New York correspondent of the San Francisco *Alta California* said the story "has set all New York in a roar." The story was quickly copied in other publications and talked about across the country. According to Twain's biographer, Albert Bigelow Paine:

> It brought the name of Mark Twain across the [Rocky] mountains, bore it up and down the Atlantic coast, and out over the prairies of the Middle West. . . . Now every one who took a newspaper was treated to the tale of the wonderful Calaveras frog, and received a mental [impression] of the author's signature. The name Mark Twain became hardly an institution, as yet, but it made a strong bid for national acceptance.[26]

A National Celebrity

As a result of his new fame, Twain was invited on the maiden voyage of the new steamer *Ajax* in its first trip to the Sandwich Islands (Hawaii). He turned down the offer because there would be no one to write his daily newspaper piece, but the idea of a journey to the islands intrigued him. He soon persuaded James Anthony and Paul Morrill at the Sacramento *Union* to send him on the *Ajax* as their special

The Story That Made Twain Famous

"Jim Smiley and His Jumping Frog" begins with a supposed meeting between Mark Twain and Simon Wheeler at a bar in Angel's Camp, California. Wheeler tells of a fellow named Jim Smiley who is showing a stranger a frog he has trained to jump:

"Maybe you understand frogs and maybe you don't understand 'em. . . . I'll [risk] forty dollars that he can outjump any frog in Calaveras County.

And the feller studied a minute, and then says, [kind of] sad-like, 'Well, I'm only a stranger here, and I ain't got no frog; but if I had frog, I'd bet you.'

And then Smiley says, 'That's all right. . . . If you'll hold my box a minute, I'll go get you a frog.' And so the feller took the box, and put up his forty dollars along with Smiley's and set down to wait.

So he set there a good while thinking and thinking to himself, and then he got the frog out and prized [pried] his mouth open and took a teaspoon and filled him full of quail-shot—filled him near up to his chin—and set him on the floor. Smiley he went to the swamp and slopped around in the mud for a long time, and finally he ketched a frog, and fetched him in, and give him to this feller, and says:

'Now, if you're ready, set him alongside of Dan'l [the frog], with his fore paws just even with Dan'l's, and I'll give the word.' Then he says, 'One—two—three—*git!*' and him and the feller touched up the frogs from behind, and the new frog hopped off lively, but Dan'l give a heave, and hysted up his shoulders . . . but it warn't no use—he couldn't budge; he was planted as solid as a church, and he couldn't no more stir than if he was anchored out. Smiley was a good deal surprised, and he was disgusted too, but he didn't have no idea what the matter was, of course. . . .

Smiley he stood scratching his head and looking down at Dan'l a long time. . . . He ketched Dan'l by the nap of the neck . . . turned him upside down and he belched out a double handful of shot. . . . He was the maddest man—he set the frog down and took out after that feller, but he never ketched him."

correspondent, writing humorous travel articles about the voyage and the islands. He sailed on the *Ajax*'s next trip and arrived in Honolulu on March 18, 1866.

The Sandwich letters were typical of his style and were well received. He was welcomed in the islands as a celebrity but became bedridden from extensive boils that flared up after a long horseback tour of the islands. Still, he continued writing. In late June he learned of the wreck of a vessel named the *Hornet*, out of New York. Fifteen passengers had survived forty-three days at sea, finally landing on the island of Hawaii. Although bedridden, Twain had himself carried on a cot to

The title page from the first edition of Twain's collection of stories.

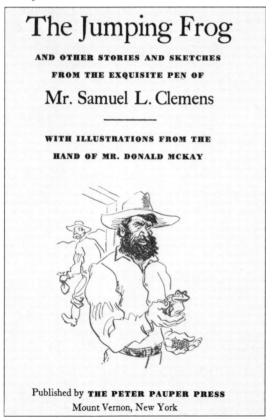

The Jumping Frog

AND OTHER STORIES AND SKETCHES
FROM THE EXQUISITE PEN OF
Mr. Samuel L. Clemens

—

WITH ILLUSTRATIONS FROM THE
HAND OF MR. DONALD MCKAY

Published by **THE PETER PAUPER PRESS**
Mount Vernon, New York

their hospital in Honolulu to get the story.

With the help of a new friend—Anson Burlingame, the U.S. ambassador to China—Twain wrote the story and sent it with a boat leaving for the States. When the article ran in the Sacramento *Union*, it was a sensation. The telegraph carried it around the country and boosted Twain's reputation even further.

Expanding Horizons

On July 27, 1866, Twain saw another lunar rainbow at sea and felt it would bring more good fortune. The fortune came, but not immediately. He was soon back in California, broke, but wanting to go to sea again. He thought of writing a book about his trip to the islands then got the idea of lecturing about it instead. Despite some earlier experience, public speaking terrified him, so he talked it over with his friend Colonel John McComb, publisher of the *Alta California*. McComb thought it was a wonderful idea. He told Twain to rent the largest hall in town and charge a dollar a ticket.

Twain made a deal with Tom Maguire, owner of the new opera house, and on October 2, 1866, he gave his first lecture. He expected to find the house empty, but it was packed. He was a public and critical success and profited four hundred dollars from the evening. It was a grand beginning to what would later become a whole new career. He was now thirty-one years old, with four professions to his credit—printer, river pilot, miner, and journalist. His confidence was overflowing. He proposed that McComb's *Alta California* finance a trip around the world.

While he waited for an answer from McComb, Twain decided to visit New York, then his family in the Midwest. On December 15, 1866, he sailed on the steamer *America*, bound for Panama. He was lucky to survive the journey. After crossing the isthmus of Panama (construction of the canal would not begin until 1904), he took the vessel *San Francisco* on to New York. Passengers died of cholera all along the journey, the last one as the New York harbor lights were in sight. Twain was spared, but shaken. He stopped in New York long enough only to say hello to Charles Henry Webb, who was putting together a collection of Twain's writings, including the jumping frog story, for publication.

McComb could not finance a world trip, so Twain considered his next career move as he visited family in Hannibal, Keokuk, and St. Louis. He still wanted to travel around the world. Then an announcement in a newspaper about the steamer *Quaker City*'s sailing for the Holy Land presented a new opportunity. He made a deal with the *Alta California:* the paper would pay for his passage, and Twain would contribute regular descriptions of the journey by letter.

The boat would leave from New York. He returned there just as his collection of stories was being published. Oddly enough, he no longer considered the issuance of his first book very important. He was more worried about a contract he made to speak at the Cooper Institute, New York's largest hall. He was terrified that no one would show.

Although the lecture hall was filled with an appreciative audience, the newspaper reviews were only "kind." The polite response made more lectures out of the question. In addition, since Twain agreed

A sign announces Twain's lecture at the Cooper Institute in New York. Although he was received by an appreciative audience, Twain's lecture received only fair reviews.

to start writing letters about his preparations, he was eighteen *Alta* letters behind, and felt he "must catch up or bust." He worked night and day to finish the letters before the boat departed.

Good Luck Abounds

The *Quaker City* left New York on June 8, 1867. The journey would prove to be the most momentous of Mark Twain's life.

The letters to the *Alta California* describing the voyage would later be edited into his first major successful book—*The Innocents Abroad*. When he returned to New York on November 19, Twain learned that his fifty-three letters to the *Alta* and six to the New York *Tribune* had expanded his celebrity into every corner of the states and territories. He wrote home that he received eighteen invitations to lecture, at one hundred dollars each, in various parts of the Union. He turned them down to continue writing letters for the *Tribune*, the New York *Citizen*, and *Galaxy*.

Twain was so popular that he traveled to Washington to try to lobby for a government job for his brother Orion, who was out of work. The officials he visited there offered *him* jobs instead, including postmaster of San Francisco. Many invited him to make after-dinner speeches.

One letter soon changed everything, and it was not one of his own. Elisha Bliss Jr., owner of the American Publishing Company in Hartford, Connecticut, offered him ten thousand dollars or 5 percent royalties if he would make a book out of his Holy Land letters. Bliss asked Twain to make the book humorous in tone. He invited Twain to a meeting in New York to arrange terms.

Mark Twain Falls in Love

Twain decided to make the trip and was able to pursue more than the book contract in New York City. On the *Quaker City* voyage he had met and become friends with eighteen-year-old Charles [Charley] Langdon. One day, in the Gulf of Smyrna (now called Gulf of Izmir, off the coast of Turkey), Charley showed Twain a minia-

---

From Mark Twain's First Lecture: October 2, 1866

The success of Twain's lectures came from his great wit and his ability to poke fun without being offensive. Consider this example, under the heading of "Native Passion for Funerals," taken from Paine's Mark Twain, A Biography:

"Big funerals are their [the Hawaiians] main weakness. Fine grave clothes, fine funeral appointments, and a long procession at things they take a generous delight in. They are fond of their chief and king; they . . . often look forward to the happiness they will experience in burying them. They will beg, borrow, or steal money enough, and flock from all the islands, to be present at a royal funeral on Oahu. Years ago a Kanaka [man] and his wife were condemned to be hanged for murder. They received the sentence with manifest satisfaction because it gave an opening for a funeral, you know. All they care for is a funeral."

The popularity of Twain's writings soon earned him numerous invitations to lecture across the United States. Over time, Twain became a skilled orator and his lectures received enthusiastic reviews.

ture photo of his sister, Olivia Langdon. Twain was thunderstruck. He spoke of the picture continuously and once even asked to borrow the locket that contained it.

When Twain went to New York City to meet Elisha Bliss Jr., he happily discovered that the Langdon family was also visiting the city. Charley Langdon wanted his family to meet the now-famous Mark Twain. So, two days before Christmas, Twain found himself having dinner across the table from Livy, the beautiful young woman whose portrait he had so admired. At thirty-two years of age he fell instantly in love.

The famous English author Charles Dickens was reading from his works that night at Steinway Hall. Twain accompanied the Langdons to the performance. Dickens might as well have been reading his grocery list. Twain could think only of Livy, sitting by his side. Within a week he visited her again at the home of a Mrs. Berry. He came at 11:00 in the morning and did not leave until midnight. He must have made a good impression on the family, for he received an open invitation to visit them at their home in Elmira, New York.

As smitten as Twain was with Olivia, other matters kept him away from her. He finished business in Washington, D.C., visited Bliss in Hartford, Connecticut, to conclude arrangements for the book, then went on to San Francisco. By the time he made it to Elmira, almost a year had passed. He came to spend only a week, but when the coach pulled out to take him to the train station, the seat came loose and he and Charley were thrown to the ground. Twain recovered in a couple of days, but ended up staying two more weeks.

He went back to lecturing, this time discussing his Holy Land trip. He was now recognized often on the street. Newspaper reviews were generally enthusiastic. Perhaps by his own design, many of the lecture stops were in central New York, giving him ample excuses to visit Elmira. When he lectured in Cleveland, Ohio, he conferred with Mary Mason Fairbanks, who had become a good friend on the *Quaker City* voyage. He told Mrs. Fairbanks that the greatest ambition in his life was to make Livy Langdon his wife.

Word of the great success of his Cleveland lecture got to Elmira quickly. As the Langdons were having breakfast one morning, Twain returned. He had already asked Livy to marry him but had been

Asking for Livy's Hand

From the beginning, Mark Twain worshiped his wife. In this excerpt from Paine's biography, Twain describes his engagement to Livy in a letter to his mother:

"She is only a little body, but she hasn't her peer in Christendom. I gave her only a plain gold engagement ring, when fashion imperatively demands a two-hundred-dollar diamond one, and told her it was typical of her future life—namely, that she would have to flourish on substance, rather than luxuries (but you see I know the girl—she don't care anything about luxuries. . . . She spends no money but her usual year's allowance, and spends nearly every cent of that on other people). She will be a good, sensible . . . wife, without any airs about her. I don't make intercession for her beforehand, and ask you to love her, for there isn't any use in that—you couldn't help it if you were to try. I warn you that whoever comes within the fatal influence of her beautiful nature is her willing slave forevermore."

Olivia Langdon, with whom Twain was immediately smitten.

told neither yes nor no. In a letter to Mrs. Fairbanks, he described "popping the question":

Dear Mother [he called her that affectionately], you are to understand that we are not absolutely engaged, because of course Livy would not fall in love Sunday & engage herself Thursday—she must have time to *prove* her heart & make *sure* that her love is permanent. . . . That she loves me I would be a fool to doubt. That she shall *continue* to love me is the thing that I must hope for & labor to secure.[27]

There was more labor called for, but not much. The Langdon family by now felt as if Mark Twain belonged to them. Livy asked her father, Jervis Langdon, to send out letters of inquiry about Twain's character. If the reports were favorable, Langdon would allow Twain to marry his daughter. Toward the end of January 1869 Twain returned from lecturing, hoping that enough letters had arrived for Mr. Langdon to make a decision.

At least one report was quite bad. One minister on the West Coast said he thought Twain would die a drunken death. Still, Mr. Langdon said "*I* believe in you. I know you better than *they* do."[28] On February 4, 1869, Samuel Langhorne Clemens and Olivia Lewis Langdon became engaged to be married.

Twain was now famous, accepted by Eastern society, and had found a woman he would love to the point of worship. He had made eight thousand dollars in his most recent lecture tour, and *The Innocents Abroad* would soon be a tremendous literary success. The book sold more than thirty-one thousand copies in its first year—Twain's decision to take royalties over a one-time ten-thousand-dollar payment had paid off. On the morning of February 2, 1870, he received a check in the mail for four thousand dollars.

That evening he and Livy were married by Hartford minister Joseph Twichell, who would become one of their best friends for the next forty years. Then they were driven to Buffalo, New York, to what Twain thought was the rented house where they would begin their marriage. Instead, they found a fully furnished, beautiful new home, complete with two servants. Livy stunned him with her explanation. "Youth [her pet name for him]," she said. "Don't you understand? It is ours, all ours—everything—a gift from father!"[29]

Samuel Clemens—now known to America as Mark Twain—had married a wonderful woman who would make him "the happiest man on Earth" and serve as his editor until the end of her days. His career was booming, and he was the owner of a brand new, fully furnished, expensive home. The newlyweds had a celebratory dinner with their guests and family, and then everyone was gone. The bride and groom were alone together, and their happiness seemed endless. As biographer Albert Bigelow Paine described it: "And so it was they entered the enchanted land."[30]

5 The Gilded Age

When Mark Twain married, he entered an age in his career that, despite some personal setbacks, could only be called golden. His and Olivia's blissful honeymoon prompted Twain to tell a friend that he felt he and Livy were living the closing chapters of a popular novel. Knowing that he had reached a great turning point, he began to reflect on his life before marriage and assess what new directions he might take. Four days after the wedding, he wrote one of the Bowen brothers—the one he had purposely caught measles from as a boy—and described what he was going through:

> I have rained reminiscences for four and twenty hours. The old life has swept before me like a panorama; the old days have trooped by in their old glory again; the old faces have looked out of the mists of the past; old footsteps have sounded in my listening ears; old hands have clasped mine, and songs I loved ages and ages ago have come wailing down the centuries.[31]

With so much happiness at home, Twain declined all offers to lecture. His father-in-law, Jervis Langdon, helped him buy into the Buffalo *Express* newspaper, and Twain worked hard at his editing and ownership duties. Life was thoroughly enjoyable, until something happend that began a string of personal calamities. Mr. Langdon became sick, and Twain and Livy dropped everything to go to Elmira to try to nurse her father back to health.

Death Casts Long Shadows

It was no use; Mr. Langdon died early in August. Partly for consolation, Livy invited Emma Nye, an old friend, to visit in Buffalo. Miss Nye caught typhoid fever while there and died in the couple's bedroom on September 29, 1870. Livy was pregnant, and the possibility of the typhoid's affecting the unborn child was a grave concern. In November a son, Langdon, was born prematurely. Then Livy soon showed symptoms of typhoid herself. Luckily, they passed.

But the family was not happy in Buffalo. The death of Emma Nye in the house troubled Livy, and with the death of her father and her own poor health, they decided it would be best to move to Elmira, to be closer to her family. They put their house up for sale, as well as Twain's share of the *Express*.

Twain and his family went to live at Quarry Farm, near Elmira, in the home

Twain's private study at Quarry Farm. Twain wrote many of his greatest works here.

of Livy's sister, Mrs. Susan Crane. Susan provided a caring atmosphere, and Livy and the baby's health improved immediately. Twain loved Quarry Farm (he would eventually write many of his greatest works there) but living there did not end the family's troubles.

On March 19, 1872, Olivia Susan was born. They called the little girl Susy, but their joy soon dampened when little Langdon died on June 2. As he had with his brother Henry, Twain blamed himself for the death. He had taken Langdon with him on a coach ride one morning to Elmira, and Langdon caught a cold that Twain was certain caused the boy's death. Langdon's loss devastated Livy. She told her sister that she felt her path through life would be lined with graves.

Writing Through the Troubles

Despite the emotional roller coaster that came with the death of Jervis Langdon, Emma Nye, and his son, Twain produced the ten pages of humor a month that he

had contracted for with a New York magazine, the *Galaxy*. In addition to the articles, Twain had been offered a book contract by Elisha Bliss to write about Twain's Far West experiences. The offer of 7.5 percent royalties was 50 percent more than he had been offered for *The Innocents Abroad*. Family woes, however, took a heavy toll; Twain quit writing for the *Galaxy* after a year. He was discouraged about the western book and made little progress. He put out a short book with Sheldon & Co., called *Mark Twain's Autobiography*, but became unhappy with it. In a year or so he bought the printer's plates and destroyed them.

Then Twain's old boss at the *Enterprise*, Joe Goodman, paid a visit and Twain reluctantly showed him what he had done on the book for Bliss. Twain did not think it was very good, but Goodman thought it was the best writing of Twain's he had seen. Publisher Bliss—who titled the book *Roughing It*—agreed. The book was a funny, fictionalized description of Twain's real-life adventures in the West.

Most of the novels that came out at this time about the West were about cowboys and Indians. *Roughing It* was different. Its descriptions of looking for gold,

An illustration from Twain's book Roughing It—*a story based on Twain's real-life adventures in the West.*

riding stagecoaches and getting in and out of trouble were so well described that the reader was taken on a grand tour of the West without actually going there. The success of the book sent Twain's public reputation soaring even higher. He received offers to write books, almanacs, articles (six thousand dollars for twelve articles from one magazine), and to lecture. He needed the money—the sale of his shares of the Buffalo *Express* had been at a loss and put him in debt. Also, his family needed a home of their own.

Career Moves

The family relocated to a suburban section of Hartford, Connecticut, called Nook Farm. A growing literary community, including Harriet Beecher Stowe, author of *Uncle Tom's Cabin*, was taking root there. Twain's minister friend, Joe Twichell, also lived there, and Elisha Bliss's publishing

A Portion of a Love Letter Home

Mark Twain never failed to stay in touch with his beloved wife. Here is an example of a letter to Livy, written from London on December 14, 1873, taken from Paine's biography:

"My own little darling, my peerless wife, I am simply mad to see you. *You* don't know how I love you—you never will. Because you do all the gushing yourself, when we are together, & so there is no use in two of us doing it—& one gusher usually silences another—but an ocean is between us now, & I *have* to gush. . . . There is no woman in the whole earth that is so lovely to me as you are, my child. You must forgive me for not talking all I feel when I am at home, honey. I *do* feel it, even if I don't talk it."

company was also in Hartford. Twain was able to get his brother Orion a job editing a Bliss-owned newspaper called *The Publisher*. Once the family was settled, Twain began lecturing again to pay off debts.

The Twain house in Hartford was popular among the literary figures who lived there. One night over dinner Twain and another writer, Charles Dudley Warner, were challenged to write a better novel than the popular social comedies their wives were reading. The result was *The Gilded Age*, which captured Washington, D.C., corruption and democracy gone hawyire. It was a success despite the Wall Street panic of September 20, 1873, which had generally affected everything in the economy. A problem arose, however, when

Harriet Beecher Stowe, author of Uncle Tom's Cabin, *was part of a literary community in Hartford, Connecticut, where Twain relocated.*

a real Eschol Sellers—the fictional name of the book's villain—appeared at the publisher's and threatened a lawsuit. The collaborators paid the man off and changed the villain's name to Beriah Sellers.

International Success and Copyright Concerns

Sales of Twain's books were heavy and his debts were soon history. His works had been translated into many languages and were popular in places as far away as Denmark. Twain's old friend, Ambassador Anson Burlingame, wrote that even the Chinese emperor had enjoyed *The Innocents Abroad*. There was only one problem with Twain's international success—copyright laws were much less strict than they are today. English versions of his books had come out with no royalty paid to him, so he decided to go to England to investigate.

The English copyright problems—which came from one thieving publisher—were not easily worked out, but his tremendous reception by the public there stunned him. His longtime friend William Dean Howells, editor of the *Atlantic Monthly* magazine and a writer, described it this way:

> In England rank, fashion, and culture rejoiced in him. Lord mayors, lord chief justices, and magnates of many kinds were his hosts; he was desired in country houses, and his bold genius captivated the favor of periodicals which spurned the rest of our nation.[32]

Twain loved every minute he spent in England but failed to come up with the book he had in mind to write about that experience. He returned to New York in late November. His great English success was reported in American periodicals, which increased his value in the eyes of prominent Americans. He realized this when he was invited to join the Lotos Club, perhaps the most prestigious organization in New York City.

By now he and Livy could afford their dream home; in addition to what Twain was making, Livy had inherited a quarter of a million dollars. They purchased five acres in Hartford that bordered a gentle stream and set about building a mansion.

While the house was being built, the family took a six-month vacation in England. This time Twain was treated like a visiting king. They met the poet Robert Browning and author Lewis Carroll. They regularly dined with English royalty. The

Twain's lectures and writings made him somewhat of a celebrity both in the United States and England.

steady social pace wore Livy down, however, so they cancelled their London engagements and visited Scotland. In Edinburgh they became great friends with Dr. John Brown, who nursed Livy back to health, and after a while the family went back to London, then to Paris for a short time.

Before sailing for America Twain delivered several lectures in London. British law held that he had to be in England when his books were published to keep the copyright, so he lectured while he waited. The lectures were more successful than anything London had ever seen. Artemus Ward had been there earlier, so the English public knew something of American humor. But the English knew Twain primarily from his writings and so were delighted when Twain could make them laugh in a theater, too.

In *The Story of English* the authors note that "Twain was the writer who brought the newly forged American language back from the frontier to the teeming cities of the East Coast."[33] They were talking about *Roughing It* and *Life on the Mississippi*. What the authors of *The Story of English* failed to note was that, with humorous lectures as well as books, Twain also took his own "American" English back to England, where the language was born, with stunning success.

The family arrived back in New York in November. Their new house in Hartford was not finished, but Twain had more pressing business. He returned to England for more lectures and received even more accolades. The Athenaeum Club made him a visiting member, an honor almost as esteemed as knighthood. The popular magazine *Punch* crowed his merits. It seemed he was more than a mere popular

Twain's ornate Victorian mansion in Hartford. This unique house became so well-known that letters addressed just to Twain—without any address—somehow made it to the author.

author: he was a major celebrity.

The family still spent summers at Livy's sister's home at Quarry Farm. Susan built a study behind the house where Twain could write, and he dearly loved working there. Everything about Quarry Farm inspired his writing. For example, one servant, a former slave called Auntie Cord, inspired Twain to write a story about her life for the prestigious *Atlantic Monthly* magazine, calling it "A True Story." The piece was a hit and, more importantly, presented one of the first memorable black heroes in American literature. Twain was then invited to contribute regularly to the magazine, and the writings he sent in were eventually fashioned into his book *Life on the Mississippi*.

351 Farmington Avenue

Meanwhile, in June 1874, a new baby whom Twain and Livy called Bay was born. She was happy and healthy, and they even-

tually named her Clara. By now the new home in Hartford was almost done. The family moved in before it was fully finished, and Twain's time was consumed with getting the construction completed. It is no wonder. Consider this description of the house:

> Mark Twain's ornate Victorian mansion in Nook Farm boasts 19 rooms, 18 fireplaces. . . . This extravaganza of intricate brickwork and trim has balconies on every side and a porch resembling a Mississippi River steamboat. The opulent interior was embellished by designer Louis Tiffany with an exotic blend of Chinese, Moorish, and American Indian motifs.[34]

The main room's fireplace featured a carved mantel imported from Scotland and a brass plate that read: "The ornament of a house is the friends that frequent it."

The new house was a magnet for visitors and strangers alike. Letters arrived addressed to "Mark Twain, United States" or

"Mark Twain, The World." One addressed "Mark Twain, God Knows Where," even made it to him. So many people wrote to Mark Twain asking for help with their manuscripts that he was forced to print and send out this reply:

> Dear Sir or Madam,—Experience has not taught me very much, still it has taught me that it is not wise to criticize a piece of literature, except to an enemy of the person who wrote it; then if you praise it that enemy admires you for your honest manliness, and if you dispraise it he admires you for your sound judgment.
>
> Yours truly,
> S.L.C.[35]

Tom Sawyer Is Born

Twain located his office in the billiard parlor on the top floor of his mansion. The room was built to resemble a pilothouse atop a steamboat. A steamboat theme was used in many parts of the house, and perhaps this inspired Twain to complete *The Adventures of Tom Sawyer*. He had begun the tale as a play, while the family summered at Saybrook, Connecticut, in 1872, and he had worked on it as a book at Quarry Farm. Now, in 1875, he finally completed it, in Hartford. For some reason, though, it was not published until December 1876.

Twain claimed that he was the first novelist to write on a typewriter and that

George the Butler

A mainstay of the Twain house at 351 Farmington Avenue in Hartford was their butler, George, a dignified black man who was with the family for decades. This story about George's character is retold by Albert Bigelow Paine in Mark Twain, A Biography:

"Clemens used to say that George came one day to wash the windows and remained eighteen years. He was precisely the sort of character that Mark Twain loved. . . . The children loved him no less than did their father. Mrs. Clemens likewise had a weakness for George, though she did not approve of him. George's morals were defective. . . . He would bet on anything, though prudently and with knowledge. . . . Mrs. Clemens' disapproval of George reached the point, now and then, where she declared he could not remain. She even discharged him once, but next morning George was at the breakfast-table, in attendance, as usual. Mrs. Clemens looked at him gravely:

'George,' she said, 'didn't I discharge you yesterday?'

'Yes, Mis' Clemens, but I knew you couldn't get along without me, so I thought I'd better stay a while.' "

An illustration from Twain's novel The Adventures of Tom Sawyer *depicts Tom and Huck, characters who have delighted readers for generations.*

Tom Sawyer was the first "type-copied" [typed from handwriting] manuscript. Whether this is true, Twain was not completely happy with the finished book. On July 5, 1875, he wrote his friend William Dean Howells: "I perhaps made a mistake in not writing it in the first person. . . . It is not a boy's book at all. It will only be read by adults. It is only written for adults."[36]

Howells did not agree with Twain's assessment of the book. He replied:

> It is altogether the best boy story I ever read. It will be an immense success, but I think you ought to treat it explicitly *as* a boy's story; grown-ups will enjoy it just as much if you do, and if you should put it forth as a story of boys' character from the grown-up point of view you give the wrong key to it.[37]

When *Tom Sawyer* came out, it was immediately popular. Its depiction of the small town of Hannibal, Tom's playing sick to escape school, Tom's pirate camp on an island, the murder of Dr. Robinson, and Tom and Becky being pursued through a dark cave by the murdering Injun Joe are adventures that have thrilled young readers for generations. Tom and

Huck's appearance at their own funeral (having been given up for lost) and Tom's thoughts about people who had wronged him are a perfect depiction of youthful emotions.

Mark Twain, Playwright

Interestingly, *Tom Sawyer* had begun as a play before being turned into a novel. Twain had a continuing interest in play writing. In 1874 he learned that an actor in San Francisco was planning to put a version of *The Gilded Age* onstage, without the author's permission. Twain telegraphed the actor, made a deal with him, and immediately wrote his own version. The actor agreed to abandon his version, for a fee. It was a wise decision. Twain's play opened in New York and made $100,000 in the next three years—the actor was paid handsomely as a result.

In the fall and winter of 1876, Twain was trying to write *Huckleberry Finn*, a sequel to *Tom Sawyer*, but was not having much luck with it. While *Huck* sat on the shelf, Twain's old friend Bret Harte came

Tom Sawyer at His Own Funeral

Wanting to know what people really thought of them, Tom Sawyer and his friends run away from home, causing the town to think they are dead. In this excerpt from Twain's The Adventures of Tom Sawyer, *they return in time to witness their own funeral:*

"As the service proceeded, the clergyman drew such pictures of the graces, the winning ways, and the rare promise of the lost lads, that every soul there, thinking he recognized these pictures, felt a pang in remembering that he had persistently blinded himself to them always before, and had as persistently seen only faults and flaws in the poor boys. The minister related many a touching incident in the lives of the departed, too, which illustrated their sweet, generous natures, and the people could easily see, now, how noble and beautiful those episodes were, and remembered with grief that at the time they occurred they had seemed rank rascalities, well deserving of the cowhide [a whipping]. The congregation became more and more moved, as the pathetic tale went on, till at last the whole company broke down and joined the weeping mourners in a chorus of anguished sobs, the preacher himself giving way to his feelings, and crying in the pulpit.

There was a rustle in the gallery, which nobody noticed; a moment later the church door creaked; the minister raised his streaming eyes above his handkerchief, and stood transfixed! First one and then another pair of eyes followed the minister's, and then almost with one impulse the congregation rose and stared while the three dead boys came marching up the aisle, Tom in the lead, Joe next, and Huck, a ruin of drooping rags, sneaking sheepishly in the rear! . . .

Tom got more cuffs [slaps] and kisses that day—according to Aunt Polly's varying moods—than he had earned before in a year; and he hardly knew which expressed the most gratefulness to God and affection for himself."

to visit in Hartford. Harte had published a very popular poem called "The Heathen Chinee" a few years earlier, and his collection of stories called *The Luck of Roaring Camp* was very popular. Harte lived in Boston now and worked on the staff of the *Atlantic Monthly* magazine with Twain's friend William Dean Howells. The *Atlantic* was the top literary magazine in the nation, and Boston critics were much more fond of Harte than of Twain.

Twain and Harte decided to collaborate on a play, *Ah Sin*. Because they were both popular, they thought it would be a great success. The play was about a funny, clever Chinese man who might have been the dramatic forefather of the film detective Charlie Chan. Despite the men's public reputations, however, the play did not do well when it opened in New York. The stress of the situation dealt what was probably the final blow to Twain and Harte's on-again, off-again friendship.

When Twain wrote his next play in 1877, *Simon Wheeler, Detective*, the actors he contacted to perform it found it faulty. He gave up play writing until 1883, when he coauthored a stage version of his book *The*

The cover of the first edition of Twain's immediately popular novel, The Adventures of Tom Sawyer.

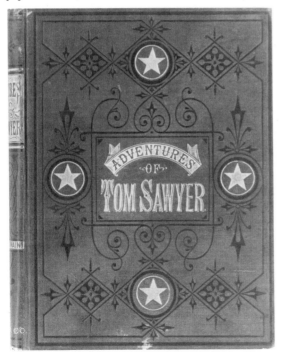

American Claimant with William Dean Howells. The play was produced in Hartford and did reasonably well, but Twain's subsequent plays of *Tom Sawyer* and *The Prince and the Pauper* were not professionally produced. In 1887 he wrote a part-English part-German play called *Meisterschaft*. It was published in the *Century Illustrated Monthly Magazine* in January 1888, but not produced. In 1899, while living in Austria, Twain translated some plays from German to English and collaborated with a writer named Siegmund Schlesinger on some original plays, but these were not produced, either. It became clear that Mark Twain would not achieve international success as a playwright.

Popularity and Problems

Dramatic success or not, the list of people who wanted Mark Twain to endorse this or that project was endless. The success of *Tom Sawyer* only escalated the number of unsolicited visitors and letters to his home in Hartford. It prompted him to remark: "The symbol of the race ought to be a human being carrying an ax, for every human being has one concealed about him somewhere, and is always seeking the opportunity to grind it."[38]

Just as he had in Virginia City and San Francisco, however, Twain was about to get himself in trouble at the peak of his popularity. Only this time it would be a speech that caused the uproar, not a published article. On December 17, 1877, Twain spoke in Boston at a dinner given by the *Atlantic* staff for John Greenleaf Whittier on the poet and editor's seventieth birthday. It was quite an occasion, and

During a dinner given for poet and editor John Greenleaf Whittier, Twain delivered a humorous sketch that characterized Oliver Wendell Holmes (left), Ralph Waldo Emerson (center), and Henry Wadsworth Longfellow (right) as rude, drunken frontier tramps. While the audience failed to get the joke, the trio was thankfully not offended.

a presitigious American literary trinity was in attendance: Oliver Wendell Holmes, Ralph Waldo Emerson, and the poet Henry Wadsworth Longfellow. Twain wrote a *Roughing It* type of sketch that characterized Holmes, Emerson, and Longfellow as rude, drunken frontier tramps who visit a young Mark Twain in a mining shack out West. Finally, the men reveal themselves to be impostors. Most of the audience failed to get the joke. Laughter was conspicuously absent. Twain was mortified. The next day, he immediately wrote letters of apology. Surprisingly, none of the men was offended. Holmes, in fact, replied that several members of his party had been quite amused. Still, given the fact that the matter had been reported widely in the papers, Twain was all but convinced his career would suffer irreparable damage.

Back in Hartford, other troubles were brewing. In September, the famous minister Henry Ward Beecher was sued by Timothy Tilton for having an adulterous affair with his wife, Elizabeth Tilton. The community and the nation were rocked by the scandal. The trouble had also caused Beecher's sister, Harriet Beecher Stowe, to descend into madness. She began letting out war whoops around the neighborhood at all hours.

In addition to Twain's professional and neighborhood problems, a national strike was taking place against the railroads, and one American political corruption scandal after another had appeared in the papers. Twain decided to take the family to Europe. The family spent a few months learning German, and in April 1878 they sailed away for an extended European vacation. The trip would result in the sighting of another lunar rainbow, another successful travel book, and a relief from the heavy costs of maintaining an expensive household.

Chapter

6 Philosopher and Publisher

The family was excited about going to Europe. Livy was especially pleased that Clara Spaulding, her lifelong friend, was going with them. Twain hired a German nurse named Rosa for his daughters to further their knowledge of German. It was clear from a notebook entry that Twain was glad to be leaving America. The entry also showed a side of him that would begin emerging more and more. Mark Twain was becoming a philosopher:

> To go abroad has something of the same sense that death brings—"I am no longer of ye; what ye say of me is now of no consequence—but of how much consequence when I am with ye and of ye. I know you will refrain from saying harsh things *because* they cannot hurt me, since I am out of reach and cannot hear them. This is why we say no harsh things of the dead." [39]

They went first to Hamburg, then to Hanover, Frankfurt, and finally to Heidelberg in May. The natural beauty of Germany was enchanting. It was a well-deserved vacation, interrupted only by a speech to American students in Heidelberg on July 4, 1878.

Twain looked forward to the arrival of his friend, Joe Twichell, who showed on August 1. Twain and Twichell immediately set off on a hike through the Black Forest and into Switzerland. Twain grew philosophical on the walks. He was strongly interested in something he called "mind telegraphy," which attempted to explain incidents that seemed like odd coincidences. He and Livy, for example, were so mentally and emotionally close that they often answered questions the other had been thinking only moments before. Twain found this also happened on his walks with the Reverend Twichell. As they walked along one mountain trail, Twichell told a story about a man he had not seen for a long time, whose whereabouts on earth he did not know. At the end of the story, Twichell looked ahead, startled. "And there's the man!" he exclaimed. The man was, amazingly, right in front of them.

On one hike Twain grew serious and confessed to Twichell that he did not believe in Christianity "at all":

> I don't believe one word of your Bible was inspired by God any more than any other book. I believe it is entirely the work of man from beginning to end—atonement and all. The problem of life and death and eternity and the true conception of God is a bigger thing than is contained in that book. [40]

To the Reverend Twichell's credit, he granted his author friend the right to believe as he wished. The subject of religion was never discussed between them again, although many of the things they talked about—problems of life and philosophy—would turn up prominently in later Twain writings (*The Mysterious Stranger* is perhaps the most notable example). None of this is to say Twain did not believe in God, however, or spiritual things. In a letter to Twichell he described his feelings about Switzerland:

> Those mountains had a soul: they thought, they spoke. . . . That stately old Scriptural wording is the right one for God's Alps and God's ocean. . . . And Lord, how pervading were the repose and peace and blessedness that poured out of the heart of the invisible Great Spirit of the mountains! [41]

By the time they got back to America, Livy had had a surprising change of heart about her religion, too. She confided on a walk with her sister that she had ceased to believe in the "orthodox Bible God." She had seen too many people in too many lands with different beliefs, she said. Now she believed in a larger God who encompassed all of creation but was not vindictive or harsh. Discussions with her husband no doubt influenced her belief. Or, perhaps, it was another example of mind telegraphy.

On the Way Home

The family spent fourteen months in Europe. They visited the great cities of Italy, with the children particularly enjoying three weeks in Venice. The winter was spent in Munich, Germany, where Twain worked on his book about their trip. In the spring, they were on to Paris, but it rained nearly every day and was distressingly

A sketch depicts Twain in a coach in Paris. Twain and his family spent fourteen months touring many sights in Europe.

foggy and chilly. The most notable thing that happened in France was that Twain gained an interest in Joan of Arc. Then they were on to England, where they made a short trip to Stratford-upon-Avon to see Shakespeare's grave.

When they were nearing New York on the return journey, Twain was standing on the ship's deck one night and saw another rare lunar rainbow. By now he was certain this was an omen of good luck. Perhaps he was right, because his greatest book— *Huckleberry Finn*—was still ahead of him.

If there were any doubt about the fame of Mark Twain by this time, it was dispelled when a customs official wanted to open Twain's baggage. Twain offered a prepared list of items he was bringing back, but the official didn't seem to believe it. The man's supervisor was summoned, who promptly told the official— "Oh, chalk his baggage, of course! Don't you know it's Mark Twain and that he'll talk all night?"[42]

Publishing Changes

From New York City, the family went directly to Quarry Farm. Twain went to work on his manuscript about their journey, called *A Tramp Abroad*. He completed it, but not without a good deal of mental turmoil about whether the book would do as well as *The Innocents Abroad*. Probably because of the success of the earlier book, *A Tramp Abroad* had sold twenty-five thousand advance copies. It came out in March of 1880 but, unfortunately, ended up selling only a third the amount of *Innocents*.

In addition, Twain was working on another book, *The Prince and the Pauper*, about a poor London boy who looks just like the reigning English prince. The boys switch places and learn what each other's life is like. Visiting Europe and England on the latest trip had inspired Twain greatly; he rushed to complete the novel once the travel book was out of the way. The girls were now eager listeners of his work, just as their mother had always been. He read the new book aloud, listening eagerly to Susy and Clara's comments and often made changes according to their reactions.

Meanwhile, in July 1880 Livy gave birth to a third little girl named Jane

An illustration from Twain's book The Prince and the Pauper. *The novel was inspired by Twain's visit to Europe and England.*

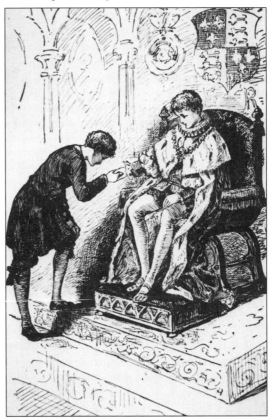

A Mississippi River Summer Sunrise

Mark Twain's fascination with the Mississippi lasted throughout his lifetime. This excerpt from his Life on the Mississippi *provides some insight:*

"First, there is the eloquence of silence; for a deep hush broods everywhere. Next, there is the haunting sense of loneliness, isolation, remoteness from the worry and bustle of the world. The dawn creeps in stealthily; the solid walls of black forest soften to gray, and vast stretches of the river open up and reveal themselves; the water is glass-smooth, gives off spectral [ghostly] little wreaths of white mist, there is not the faintest breath of wind, nor stir of leaf; the tranquility is profound and infinitely satisfying. Then a bird pipes up, another follows, and soon the pipings develop into a jubilant riot of music."

The sun rises over the scenic Mississippi River.

Lampton after her grandmother. Almost immediately, however, they began calling her Jean. To her father's amusement, Jean soon became the favorite person on the older girls' affection list, followed by Livy, the cats Motley and Fraulein, then him.

When *The Prince and the Pauper* was complete, Twain changed publishers. Elisha Bliss at the American Publishing Company had died after a long illness, but before dying had urged Twain to seek other publishers. Twain's friend William Dean Howells recommended James R. Osgood's company as publisher. Osgood loved *The Prince and the Pauper* and put it out with lavish illustrations. The only hitch came when the book was published in Canada. Twain was forced to go there, in the middle of winter, to satisfy Canadian copyright law, which required an author to be in that country when a book was published.

By December 1881 the book was available in America, Canada, Denmark, and Germany. Twain dedicated it to his young editors: "To those good-mannered and agreeable children, Susy and Clara

Clemens." The book was well received, but the public was a bit confused. They were used to humor and jokes from Mark Twain; this was simply a beautiful, well-crafted story with a moral. The reviewer from the New York *Herald*, however, said the book was a logical step in the progress of Twain's writings:

> Through all his publications may be traced the marks of the path which has led up to this happy height. His humor has often been the cloak, but not the mask, of a sturdy purpose. His work has been characterized by a manly love of truth, a hatred of humbug, and a scorn for cant [conventional, trite, or unconsidered opinions]. . . . The character of these two boys, twins in spirit, will rank with the purest and loveliest creations of child-life in the realm of fiction.[43]

Wrestling with the Masterpiece

Once *The Prince and the Pauper* was finished, Twain turned his attention back to a book he did not like nearly as much, *The Adventures of Huckleberry Finn*. Writing *Huckleberry Finn* caused its author as much trouble as Huck caused the adults in the book. It would eventually take him eight years to complete.

The name Huckleberry came from the Hartford area. He had first learned about huckleberries there, and he loved the sound of the word. "I never saw any place where morality and huckleberries flourished as they do here,"[44] he had said in a letter after his first visit with Elisha Bliss.

Huckleberry also had another meaning—in slang, it meant a person of no consequence, which no doubt reminded Twain of Jimmy Finn, the Hannibal town drunk. Inspirations aside, the story was timeless. Like Tom Blankenship, who was his model, Huck Finn was like a force of nature—wild, free to come and go as he pleased, untamed by civilization. Huck did everything proper boys were forbidden. He drank, smoked tobacco, and swore. He was always getting into trouble. Tom Sawyer had his Aunt Polly to keep him in line; Huck had no one. But for all his faults, Huck was good at heart and in the

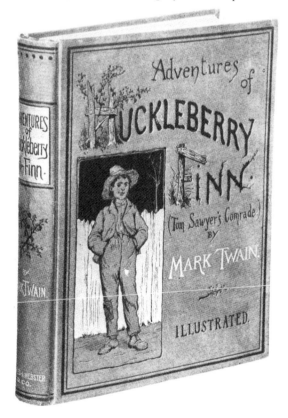

A cover from the first edition of Twain's novel The Adventures of Huckleberry Finn. *This sequel to* Tom Sawyer *took Twain eight years to complete.*

end came out on top.

Twain must have realized that the book, for all its troubles, was going to sell well. He began to think about publishing alternatives. In 1878, Twain had published a book of writings with Osgood and Company called *The Stolen White Elephant*. Then came *The Prince and the Pauper* in 1881, followed in 1883 by *Life on the Mississippi*, the book about Twain's days as a river pilot. *Life on the Mississippi* was a huge success, a worldwide triumph. Emperor William of Germany, for example, said it was his favorite book. With that sort of popularity in mind, Twain began thinking about better business arrangements. When he finally finished *Huckleberry Finn* in 1883, he realized that he might make more money if he published the book himself.

His niece's husband, Charles L. Webster, had learned the business of selling books by subscription while working with Osgood. Subscription book selling worked the way magazines do today; people agreed to buy a book before it was published, usually based on the author's reputation. Selling a new Mark Twain book was, by this time, a guarantee of success. So, with Twain as general director, Charles L. Webster & Co., publishers, was born in 1884.

Censorship

Webster found a wonderful new illustrator named E.W. Kemble for *Huck Finn*. To help sell the book, an excerpt appeared in the December issue of *Century* magazine. The editor of *Century*, Richard Watson Gilder, wrote Twain that the excerpt was the most finished and condensed writing he had done, and as dramatic and power-ful an episode as he knew of in literature. Still, Gilder removed references to nakedness, dead cats, and other subjects considered unsavory. For example, Huck says "nigger woman," and Gilder changed it to "one of the servants." "In a sweat" became "in a hurry." *Life*, a new literary magazine, attacked the book for its gutter realism and called it unsuitable for young people. Critics who liked the genteel *Prince and the Pauper* were appalled.

It didn't matter. Critical opinion and public opinion rarely agree when it comes to ground-breaking works of art. By early

An illustration by E.W. Kemble depicts the adventurous Huck proudly displaying his prize from a successful hunt.

What Ever Happened to Huck Finn?

No sequel to Huckleberry Finn *was ever published. Huck himself tells us why at the end of the book,* The Adventures of Huckleberry Finn. *The scene begins as Jim explains what happened to Huck's drunken, outlaw father:*

"Jim says, kind of solemn: 'He ain't a-comin' back no mo', Huck.'

I says: 'Why, Jim?'

'Nemmine [never mind] why, Huck—but he ain't comin' back no mo'.'

But I kept at him; so at last he says:

'Doan' [don't] you 'member de house dat was float'n down de river, en dey wuz a man in dah [there], kivered [covered] up, en I went in en unkivered him and didn't let you come in? Well, den, you kin git you' money when you wants it, kase [because] dat wuz him.'

Tom's well now, and got his bullet [from being wounded] around his neck on a watch-guard [chain] for a watch, and is always seeing what time it is, and so there ain't nothing more to write about, and I am rotten glad of it, because if I'd 'a' knowed what a trouble it was to make a book I wouldn't 'a' tackled it, and ain't a-going to no more."

1885 Webster had amassed fifty thousand advance orders for the book, and it was a runaway success. Still, Mark Twain was stung by the fault-finding comments. It would be almost five years before he published another book of his own.

Surprisingly, the censorship that *Huck Finn* bore when it first came out reappears today, but for different reasons. In the 1980s it was banned from some high school libraries because terms like Nigger Jim were considered racist.

Despite its problems, *Huck* has more than stood the test of time. The book's influence carries forward today. Many film versions have been made—the latest in 1993. A Broadway musical version, *Big River*, with music by Roger Miller, was a smash success. In 1986 Roy Harvey Pearce, professor of American and English literature at the University of California, San Diego, had this to say about Huck Finn:

He is so powerfully a being of truth as against conscience, self as against society, that he exists not as an actuality but as a possibility. In him Mark Twain projects the American's sense that somewhere, at some point—even if only in the imagination—it would be possible to regain access to the truth, if only we could cut through the shams of conscience and of the institutions that form and justify it.[45]

A Publishing Fortune Is Made

Huckleberry Finn was controversial and successful, but it was not the greatest success of Mark Twain's new publishing company. That came when he and Webster published a book written by a president of the United States. In 1879, Twain gave a speech at a dinner for former president Ulysses S. Grant, whom he had interviewed for a periodical twelve years before. In 1880 Grant came to Hartford to speak on behalf of James A. Garfield, who was running for election. Since Hartford was situated halfway between Boston and New York, it was considered an important

Twain persuaded former president Ulysses S. Grant to write his memoirs for Twain's publishing company. Grant died just three days after he finished the book, which went on to be a huge success.

city. Twain again gave a speech that Grant enjoyed, and Grant's son dined at Twain's house.

Twain helped campaign for Garfield for president and later used his influence with Garfield. For example, he wrote Garfield on behalf of black leader Frederick Douglass, to keep Douglass from losing his job as U.S. marshal of the District of Columbia. When Garfield was assassinated in the summer of 1881, however, Twain's political influence appeared to be gone. When Chester A. Arthur became president, William Dean Howells's father wrote to Howells, expressing concern that Arthur might replace him as consul at Toronto. Howells contacted Twain, and together they paid a call on former president Grant, hoping to influence him to put in a good word with Arthur. Only a month before, Twain had addressed the cadets at West Point with Grant and some others and was on fine terms with the former president and war hero.

The meeting was a triumph. Grant would meet with the new president soon and agreed to speak to him on behalf of Howells's father. Also, Twain first suggested that Grant write his memoirs for publication. Grant didn't think he could write a good book or that it would sell. Twain said:

> I argued that the book would have an enormous sale, and that out of my experience I could save him from making unwise contracts with publishers, and would have the contract arranged for him in such a way they could not swindle him, but he said he had no necessity for any addition to his income.[46]

Several years would pass before Grant finally agreed to do the book, and even

A Letter to the President

Twain was supportive of anyone in need of help. He wrote to President Garfield on behalf of black rights activist Frederick Douglass. This excerpt is taken from Paine's biography:

"A simple citizen may express a desire, with all propriety, in the matter of recommendation to office, and so I beg permission to hope that you will retain Mr. Douglass in his present office of Marshal of the District of Columbia, if such a course will not clash with your own preferences or with the expediencies and interests of your Administration. I offer this petition with peculiar pleasure and strong desire, because I so honor this man's high and blemishless character, and so admire his brave, long crusade for the liberties and elevation of his race."

then Twain almost lost the contract. He was visiting with Grant in 1885 when he learned that Grant had been offered a publishing contract with the *Century*. Grant had lost his entire fortune due to the swindles of a business partner. He was quite broke and needed the money. Twain reminded Grant of his previous offer and advice, and Grant realized that Twain should have the book. Twain wrote Grant a check for twenty-five thousand dollars that day, and the deal was done.

Grant's *Memoirs* were not easy to complete. The man was dying of tongue cancer. Twain was greatly saddened by his friend's deteriorating condition and amazed at the persistence and energy the former president was able to put into the book. At first Grant wrote in longhand, then he worked with a stenographer.

Three days after Grant finished his book, he was dead. All the nation mourned.

Three hundred thousand copies of the two-volume set of *Memoirs* had been sold. The first royalty check written to Mrs. Grant by Charles L. Webster & Co. on February 27, 1886, was for $200,000. It was the largest royalty check in history, and Mrs. Grant eventually made nearly $450,000 from the venture.

By the time the book was published, Mark Twain was fifty. Life was going along well. Too well, perhaps. Twain said he was frightened at the proportions of his prosperity, that whatever he touched turned to gold. Would that it had remained so forever. Though he was then basking in the sunshine of prosperity, Twain inevitably experienced a reversal of fortune.

Chapter

7 A Connecticut Yankee's Misfortunes

In addition to being an author, lecturer, and publisher, Mark Twain also pursued inventing. For example, he came up with a self-adjusting pants suspender. Another invention that sold well was "Mark Twain's Scrapbook" that featured strips of dried glue on its pages that could be moistened to paste on a scrapbook item.

Twain spent fortunes that he never got back on other people's ideas as well. He invested in a "guaranteed energy-saving" steam generator that was a total loss. He wasted thirty-two thousand dollars in sixteen months on a new steam pulley. He sank twenty-five thousand dollars into a new marine telegraph, wasted time and money with a watch company, and had a similar misadventure with an accident insurance company.

Then along came a man who might have made Twain a billionaire, but Twain was sick of bad investments and would barely even listen to him. The man's name was Alexander Graham Bell, and his invention was the telephone. At least Twain did not hold a grudge. When the telephone became available for use, he installed one in his home that connected to the Hartford *Courant* newspaper. He bragged about it, claiming to be the first person in the world to install a telephone in a private house.

The Press He Should Have Skipped

With his predisposition toward new inventions, Twain invested five thousand dollars in 1880 in a typesetting machine created

A then-unknown inventor named Alexander Graham Bell wanted Twain to invest in his machine— the telephone. Twain, however, had already lost thousands in bad investments and refused to back Bell.

by James Paige. The machine was being assembled at the Colt Arms factory in Hartford. Twain initially called Paige a genius; what he may have called him at the end of their association is probably not printable. By 1885 Paige had become almost solely dependent on Twain for funds to live and to continue working on the machine. By 1890 Twain was writing almost nothing and devoting most of his time to promoting the Paige "compositor" to the world.

Twain's reputation brought some interest from other investors, at least. Bram Stoker, the author of *Dracula*, sent Twain a check for $100 to invest in the Paige machine. By the time that check arrived, however, the cause was lost, and Twain knew it. He returned Stoker's money, and that of many other investors. By 1891 the Paige project was eating up $5,000 a month from Twain's accounts. It was standard talk around the house among Twain's daughters that certain things could not be afforded because "the machine" wasn't done. The venture was a more colossal blunder than not investing in Alexander Graham Bell's telephone. The $190,000 Twain eventually pumped into the machine would result in the bankruptcy of his and Webster's company.

Paralleling the development of Paige's machine was the Mergenthaler linotype, which eventually set the standard for printing equipment of the era. While Paige tinkered with his machine, which had twenty thousand parts and never seemed quite right, the much simpler Mergenthaler typesetting equipment got a lot of attention. The New York *Tribune* ordered twenty-three linotypes, tried them out, and was pleased. When the promoters of the Mergenthaler offered to exchange half their shares for half of Twain's shares

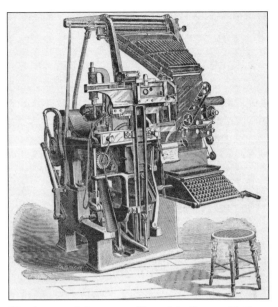

Twain turned down an offer to join forces with the promoters of the Mergenthaler linotype machine, a decision that probably cost him huge sums of money.

in the Paige machine, he shortsightedly decided the offer was a sign of weakness on their part and turned them down.

It was another amazing blunder. In short order the eccentric Paige decided he needed two million dollars to properly fund his machine. Twain enlisted the aid of his old editor friend Joe Goodman in securing western mining millionaires to invest, but none came through. Even Henry Huddleston Rogers, a multimillionaire investor in the Standard Oil Company who became Twain's financial advisor, could raise few funds for the Paige compositor.

In March 1893, after a long time with the family in Europe, Twain traveled back to America, hoping for better news about the Paige machine. He went to New York and Chicago, investigating Paige's promises of imminent wealth. As usual, prospects looked good, but by August

Paige had managed to wreck Twain's hopes again.

Ironically, the Mergenthaler Company eventually bought all rights to the Paige machine for twenty thousand dollars and gave it as a gift to the Sibley College of Engineering. Sibley exhibited it as the most costly piece of machinery for its size that was ever constructed.

Ups and Downs

On October 27, 1890, Twain's mother died after a long illness. Not long after that, Livy's mother died also—on Livy's birthday. Then another member of their extended family died. Livy felt a sense of dread, as if more trouble were just around the corner. Toward the end of December Twain wrote his publishing manager: "Merry Christmas to you, and I wish to God I could have one myself before I die."[47]

Perhaps the floods of money Twain lost on the Paige typesetter drove him to distraction. He became involved with all manner of nonproductive activities that pulled him away from the true source of his fortune—namely, his books and lectures. For example, he became captivated by a technique in which the mind cures physical ailments called a "mind cure" and soon had his whole family involved with it. He also held regular meetings to discuss the poetry of Robert Browning at length. Another wild scheme was a short campaign to get Christopher Columbus's bones buried beneath the Statue of Liberty. Not long after that, he chanced upon Professor Loisette's School of Memory— "The Instantaneous Art of Never Forget-

The failure of the Paige typesetter left Twain distracted and deeply in debt.

ting"— in New York. Twain came to believe so much in the professor that he wrote a letter of recommendation that was used to promote the memory technique far and wide. (Later he became disenchanted and withdrew his endorsement.)

No matter what wild idea Mark Twain came up with, the continual visitors and social invitations did not lessen. Nor did the expenses that came with such an active social life. Twain met other famous writers, such as Robert Louis Stevenson, author of *Treasure Island.* He dined at the White House regularly with President and Mrs. Grover Cleveland. He helped found the famous Players' Club in New York City. In 1888 he was awarded an honorary master of arts degree from Yale University. Life was continuously played out in the public eye, only the public did not know of Twain's perilous financial problems.

Nor did it know of his other problems, of a physical nature. Twain was troubled so badly with rheumatism in his right arm and shoulder that he and Livy planned a trip to several healing spas in Europe for relief. By May 1891 Twain's trouble with his writing arm was so acute that he alternated using a pen with speaking into a cylinder phonograph. He also worked at writing with his left hand.

Physical ailments plagued the rest of the family as well. Livy was diagnosed with heart disease. Jean developed an odd personality change and was diagnosed as having epilepsy.

The house at Nook Farm was now impossible to keep up; expenses were simply too great. On the sixth of June the family sailed for Europe, not knowing that it would be nine years before they all returned. As a family, they would never again live at that magnificent dwelling in Hartford.

On a brighter note the Twains were in great demand at European social occasions. That winter in Berlin Twain had dinner with the German emperor. His cousin had married a German, von Versen, who became a high-ranking general. This connection, combined with Twain's own celebrity, got him and his family invited to all diplomatic events. Unfortunately, association with royalty and high society did nothing for their financial worries.

Writing Despite the Troubles

In an attempt to build on earlier success, in 1889 Twain began a sequel to *Huckleberry Finn* called *Huck Finn and Tom Sawyer Among the Indians*. He never completed it. With creditors closing in, he was again almost solely dependent on his writing for income. In 1891 he turned his old play *The American Claimant* into a book and sold the syndication rights for twelve thousand dollars to the McClure Syndicate. The book was later published by Charles L. Webster & Co.

After getting relief from his rheumatism at European health spas like Aix-les-Bains, Twain returned to writing with his right hand. To his credit, he wrote with his old energy most times, if on a lower literary level. He continued publishing letters and articles in various periodicals. In 1892 he wrote *Tom Sawyer Abroad* and *The Tragedy of Pudd'nhead Wilson*, which were serialized in 1893 in *St. Nicholas* and *Century* magazines, respectively. (Pudd'nhead Wilson, a detective considered an idiot until he uses fingerprinting to show the true identity of twins, greatly helped popularize that new science.)

Publishing Rises and Falls

The fantastic success of Grant's *Memoirs* had quite an effect on the marketplace. The public was anxious to read anything of a true military nature. Charles L. Webster & Co. also put out books by Union generals George McClellan and Sam W. Crawford, and Twain's future as a publisher looked very promising. Then he and Charley Webster came up with the idea of publishing a book by the pope—*The Life of Pope Leo XIII*—and Charley and his wife Annie traveled to Rome to meet the pontiff. They calculated to sell at least 100,000 copies of the book to loyal

Catholics everywhere.

All of the books Webster published were profitable, but no book sold with the same runaway success as the Grant memoirs had. The pope's book turned a modest profit, and nothing more. An unfortunate blunder for the company was that for four years no one in the company—Twain in particular—thought to concentrate on the company's main strength—namely, the books of Mark Twain. *Huck Finn* came out in 1884; it had been eight years in the writing, and perhaps the process of getting it done simply wore Twain out. *A Connecticut Yankee in King Arthur's Court* was not published until December 1889.

Whatever the explanation, *Connecticut Yankee* was a good book, and sold fairly well. In the story, fictional hero Hank Morgan is a foreman at the Colt Arms factory where the Paige compositor is being built. (Perhaps that gives us a clue as to just how much of Twain's thought and energy went into James Paige's invention.) It was another historical novel: Morgan travels back through time to Camelot and uses "Yankee ingenuity" to help free King Arthur and his court from the evil influence of Merlin the magician.

When *Yankee* was published, many of Twain's friends, including William Dean Howells, loved the book. It was a great tale of man's inhumanity to man and spoke against human injustice. That was in America, however. Because the book was set in England, the great majority of English critics were sorely offended. *Connecticut Yankee* was an attack on the monarchy, they said, that most ancient of English institutions. One critic called the book a lamentable failure, while another said it was audacious sacrilege.

Twain's fellow writers came to his de-

An illustration from Twain's book A Connecticut Yankee in King Arthur's Court. *While the book was praised by many American readers, it was attacked by English critics.*

fense. Andrew Lang said in the *Illustrated London News* that he had not read *Connecticut Yankee*, but that *Huckleberry Finn* was a masterpiece that "cultured critics" could not appreciate.

An Encounter with Kipling

In the summer of 1889 a young man making a tour around the world had sought out Twain at the family's summer residence in Elmira, New York. His name was Rudyard Kipling. Kipling was not yet

What Upset the English Critics

This speech of Hank Morgan's, from A Connecticut Yankee in King Arthur's Court, *speaks of timeless truths. For those blindly loyal to authority, it is upsetting reading material:*

"You see my kind of loyalty was loyalty to one's country, not to its institutions or its office-holders. The country is the real thing, the substantial thing, the eternal thing; it is the thing to watch over, and care for, and be loyal to; institutions are extraneous, they are its mere clothing, and clothing can wear out, become ragged, cease to be comfortable, cease to protect the body from winter, disease, and death. To be loyal to rags, to shout for rags, to worship rags, to die for rags—that is a loyalty of unreason, it is pure animal; it belongs to monarchy, was invented by monarchy; let monarchy keep it."

Rudyard Kipling visited Twain at his Elmira residence during the English author's world tour. Twain was impressed by Kipling, who would later write a critique of Connecticut Yankee.

famous, but Twain was impressed with him. "He is a most remarkable man," Twain said. "Between us we cover all knowledge; he knows all that can be known, and I know the rest."[48] When *Connecticut Yankee* came out, Kipling wrote a critique:

> Oh shame! Oh shock! Oh fie! I have been reading the new book which you also will have read by this time—the book about the yankee animal in the court yard. It's * * * [curses] but I don't believe he ever wrote it; or, if he did, I am certain that if you held it up to a looking glass or picked out every third word or spelled it backward you would find that it hid some crystal clean tale as desirable as Huck Finn.[49]

But all this was before the Paige typesetter sucked Twain's finances down an endless drain. When he made it back to New York at the end of August 1893, Twain was fifty-eight years old and burdened with a $160,000 debt. He had no good idea of

Some Pudd'nhead Wilson Maxims

These quotes come from the "Pudd'nhead Wilson's Calendar," where Pudd'nhead's maxims are quoted:

"It takes your enemy and your friend, working together, to hurt you to the heart; the one to slander you and the other to get the news to you."

"Consider well the proportions of things. It is better to be a young June-bug than an old bird of paradise."

"When angry, count four; when very angry, swear."

"Truth is mighty and will prevail. There is nothing the matter with this, except that it ain't so."

"There is an old-time toast which is golden for its beauty. 'When you ascend the hill of prosperity may you not meet a friend.'"

"Training is everything. The peach was once a bitter almond; cauliflower is nothing but cabbage with a college education."

"Adam was but human—this explains it all. He did not want the apple for the apple's sake, he wanted it only because it was forbidden. The mistake was in not forbidding the serpent; then he would have eaten the serpent."

how to handle it. One night Dr. Clarence C. Rice, a friend of Twain, introduced him to Henry Huddleston Rogers. Rogers had seen Twain lecture about the Sandwich Islands years before. He said that since then he had read everything of Twain's he could find. They became friends instantly, and Dr. Rice asked Rogers to help Twain with his finances, which Rice said were "a good deal confused."

Rogers took on the task gladly. Meanwhile, Twain was again the toast of New York, lauded wherever he went. Twain's spirits again soared. He wrote Livy of his good fortune in meeting Rogers. Also, the *Pudd'nhead Wilson* serialization in the *Century* was proving popular. One could hear Pudd'nhead's maxims, or sayings, quoted in the street. It seemed the old Twain luck had returned. But he had been so long in Europe that he had overlooked terrible economic conditions in America, and he turned down offers to lecture for money. On June 27, 1893, the United States experienced a stock market crash. By year's end six hundred banks had closed, seventy-four railroads had gone out of business, and more than fifteen thousand commercial businesses had collapsed. It was the worst depression the country had ever seen.

Multimillionaire oil magnate Henry Huddleston Rogers agreed to help Twain with his finances, which were in shambles. Once the depression hit, however, there was little Rogers could do to help.

By April 16, 1894, the Webster publishing company was deep in trouble. Publishing manager Fred J. Hall arrived at Twain's room at the Players' Club in New York City and told him that the Mount Morris Bank's new board of directors wanted ten thousand dollars within a few days or they would foreclose on the company. Twain got Rogers to intervene, but there was only so much the man could do. He arranged for Twain to turn his copyrights over to Livy (she was owed sixty thousand dollars by Twain's company, and so foreclosed to keep the copyrights in the family). The home in Hartford was, thankfully, already in her name. The creditors

backed off, but Charles L. Webster & Co. was forced to close its doors on April 18. An interesting, little known fact may have saved Twain's company and serves to show that Twain may have compromised his high principles for Rogers. An author brought Webster & Co. an expose on the criminal activities of high-ranking members of the Standard Oil Company. (John D. Rockefeller, the founder of the company, was repored to have had people killed to protect his interests.) This was before Ida Tarbell's expose—*The History of the Standard Oil Company*—was published in 1907. Twain turned the book down, in deference to Rogers. Might it have brought about a public uproar and sold well? We will never know.

The closure of Mark Twain's firm was big news across a nation already full of woe. Twain swore he would pay back every penny owed, and sympathy poured in. Friends sent money, which he proudly returned. Though the bankruptcy was regrettable, at least holding off debtors gave him and his family some temporary mental relief. Twain returned to Europe and his wife and children and continued work on his new book, *Personal Recollections of Joan of Arc*, a fictional biography of the French heroine and martyr.

Paying It All Back

In 1894 finances were sufficiently bad that all Twain could give his wife on their twenty-fifth wedding anniversary was a silver five-franc piece. It was quite a step down for a family that had once spent $100,000 in one year for household expenses. But though Mark Twain was down, he certainly wasn't out. The manner in which he recovered his fortune prompted steel magnate and friend Andrew Carnegie to remark that Twain entered a fiery furnace a man and emerged a hero.

In 1895 Twain completed his *Joan of Arc* book, as well as *Tom Sawyer, Detective.* The former was one of Twain's great works; the latter played on the popularity of Sherlock Holmes books and was simply good entertainment. Both would be published in 1896. They were good books, but not de-signed to handle Twain's debts. *Joan of Arc* was unique in one fashion. It was the only one he felt worthy of dedication to Livy:

1870   TO MY WIFE   1895
OLIVIA LANGDON CLEMENS
THIS BOOK
is tendered on our wedding anniversary in grateful recognition of her twenty-five years of valued service as my literary adviser and editor.

THE AUTHOR[50]

A Portion of a Twain Lecture

Twain delivered an address to an Army and Navy Club dinner in New York City in 1886. The subject was "General Grant's Grammar." The portion below, taken from Paine's biography, shows Twain's wit, as well as an ability to emotionally move an audience:

"There is that about the sun which makes us forget his spots, and when we think of General Grant our pulses quicken and his grammar vanishes; we only remember that this is the simple soldier who, all untaught of the silken phrase-makers, linked words together with an art surpassing the art of the schools and put into them a something which will still bring to American ears, as long as America shall last, the roll of his vanished drums and the tread of his marching hosts. What do we care of grammar when we think of those thunderous phrases, 'Unconditional and immediate surrender,' 'I propose to move immediately upon your works,' 'I propose to fight it out on this line if it takes all summer.'. . . That last phrase is not strictly grammatical, and yet it did certainly wake up this nation as a hundred million tons of A-number-one fourth-proof, hard-boiled, hide-bound grammar from another mouth could not have done. And finally we have that gentler phrase, that one which shows you another true side of the man, shows you that in his soldier heart there was room for other than gory war mottoes and in his tongue the gift to fitly phrase them: 'Let us have peace.'"

To fulfill his promise to pay all the creditors of his publishing company and restore his family to comfort, Twain went back to the lecture platform in July 1895. He was almost sixty but was determined to spend a year on a round-the-world campaign. In the years since quitting lecture tours, before the financial troubles, he had made an occasional speech here and there—but never for money. He did not much like lecturing. Among other reasons, it took him away from home. The fact of the matter was, though, that he had turned down a lot of money by not lecturing. A Mark Twain appearance would draw in one thousand dollars or more a night, a princely sum in those days.

Now he *had* to lecture, and he went at it like a whirlwind. He lectured across the United States, up into Canada, then on to Australia, New Zealand, India, and South Africa. Everywhere he went audiences thronged to see the famous man and repeatedly gave him standing ovations. In July 1896, he arrived in England triumphant, hoping to take six months and write a book called *Following the Equator* about his journey.

Following the death of his daughter Susy, Twain fell into a depression. He became bitter and critical toward life and the human race in general.

The Death of Susy

The plan was interrupted in devastating fashion. In August a crushing emotional blow came by cable. Susy Clemens, only twenty-four, had died in Hartford of meningitis. As with deaths of other dearly beloved people in his past, Twain was so devastated he felt he could barely go on. He wrote Livy on August 26:

> I know what misery is, at last, my darling. I know what I shall suffer when you die. I see, now, that I have never known sorrow before, but only some poor modification of it. In Henry's case I would not allow myself to think of my loss, lest the burden be too heavy to bear; but in poor Susy's case I have no disposition or desire to put it out of my mind—I seem to want to think of it all the time. For the present the zest of life is gone from me.[51]

The family spent the winter in England. Despite the success of his world tour, Twain now became bitter because of Susy's death. He became critical toward life and the human race in general. "Man is the only animal that blushes, or needs to," he wrote.[52] Like the minister extolling the virtues of the boys given up for dead in *Tom Sawyer*, Twain went through a period of "what if" about his relationship with Susy. He wrote Reverend Twichell:

> But I have this consolation: that dull as I was I always knew enough to be proud when she commended me or my work—as proud as if Livy had done it herself—& I took it as the accolade from the hand of genius. I see now—as Livy always saw—that she had greatness in her, & that she herself was dimly conscious of it.
>
> And now she is dead—& I can never tell her.[53]

Through the support of his friends and remaining daughters, and with Livy's calm, sure guidance, Twain eventually returned to his work. Working may have saved his life, so great was his depression and rage over Susy's death. At the end of October he wrote the first chapter of *Following the Equator*.

Though Twain would not again write a book to equal *Huck Finn*, or even *Yankee*, he still had a great deal to contribute to the world. Biographer Justin Kaplan called the next four years of Twain's life "The Dark Side of the Moon." Kaplan also made the accurate observation that Mark Twain, in paying off his debts in such an honorable way, was now the stuff of legend. He was known and loved literally around the globe. Despite his personal troubles Mark Twain was at that time the most conspicuous person on the planet.

Chapter

8 To a Person Sitting in Darkness

In 1897 a newspaper published an article stating that Mark Twain was living in poverty, abandoned by his family. It was a total lie, but the family had certainly abandoned all hopes of living in Hartford again. Since Susy had died in the house, Livy could scarcely bear the thought of re-

A Life *magazine cover pays tribute to Twain— revered author and American hero. Twain's colorful writings became a regular feature in American magazines.*

turning there. Instead, they spent the next few years in England and Europe. During their "exile," as Twain called it, he and his family dined with kings, queens, and emperors on a frequent basis.

He contributed regularly to American magazines during this period, writing with a great deal of humor and insight about whatever he was doing. Everywhere they went he was recognized and given privileges afforded very few. He even spoke by invitation to the English House of Lords regarding his views on copyright laws.

Following the Equator had sold thirty thousand copies quickly, and Henry Huddleston Rogers was doing a tremendous job of managing Twain's accounts. At the end of January 1898 Twain made the final payment on his debts. He had given himself five years to pay everything off; he achieved the objective in less than three. The accomplishment made newspaper headlines across the world, and editorials called him a hero. From October 1898 to April 1899 Twain's money more than doubled. Livy calculated that they still owned the house in Hartford and had $107,000 cash in the bank, with regular, handsome royalty checks coming in.

By then they were living in expensive hotels in Vienna, and Twain was writing with his old authority. Perhaps his very best short story, "The Man That Corrupted Hadleyburg," was written during this time and published in *Harper's Weekly* magazine.

By the middle of 1900 the family was living at Dollis Hill House, a tranquil, beautiful place just outside London. It had been the favorite residence of the English politician and prime minister, Gladstone, and has since been turned into Gladstone Park. The family loved Dollis Hill so much they did not want to leave, but the call of home was too strong. On October 6 they sailed for America aboard the *Minnehaha*.

Mark Twain, Crusader

The public reception Mark Twain received in Europe was nothing compared to the one he received in America. Reporters surrounded him the minute he stepped off the ship in New York on November 15. Twain was thrilled to be back. He joked to reporters: "If I ever get ashore I am going to break both of my legs so I can't get away again."[54]

Twain and his family settled into a house at 14 West Tenth Street in New York City. The newspapers immediately alerted the public to Twain's whereabouts. So many people came calling—the majority of them unknown to Twain—that he had to hire a private secretary. Reporters would not leave him alone, for Twain's comments always made good reading. Sometimes they invented things he supposedly said without even speaking to him.

He spoke at so many dinners that he wore himself to a frazzle before friends urged him to slow down. It was hard to turn down invitations; the events were exciting. At one dinner, for example, he introduced English war hero Winston Churchill.

As Twain was heard, at dinners and in print, the public began to realize that a change was taking place. This was a new Mark Twain. The old humor was still there, but a new social consciousness—a biting edge even—was equally prominent.

A significant change in his career oc-

Twain and Russian author Maxim Gorky are honored at a New York banquet. Twain exhausted himself by accepting many invitations to speak at dinners and other events.

curred at this point, coinciding with the change in American focus from western expansion to the country's place in the world. On July 12, 1893, historian Frederick Jackson Turner had written that the West was now "closed." In his essay, "The Significance of the Frontier in American History," Turner said:

> To the frontier the American intellect owes its striking characteristics. That coarseness and strength . . . acuteness and inquisitiveness, that practical, inventive turn of mind . . . restless, nervous energy . . . that buoyancy and exuberance which comes with freedom.[55]

Those "striking characteristics" might well have been a description of Mark Twain. Audiences and admirers on his world tour had repeatedly told Twain that he epitomized America in spirit. He was sixty-five now. Just as America was no longer driven by the promise of free land and great riches on its frontier, in 1900 Twain was more interested in American politics and world affairs than life on Huck Finn's Mississippi River or in the Nevada Territory of *Roughing It*.

Attacking Social Injustices

America was now a world power, maybe the greatest power on earth. American armies had made Cuba free, taken the Philippines from Spain, and helped crush a rebellion against foreigners in China. Twain's Sandwich Islands were now Hawaii and had become part of the United States, as had Puerto Rico. America was proud of its expanding role in world affairs. And Mark Twain, America's most influential celebrity, was a citizen of the world, not just the United States. He was not a politician and had no plans to be one, but when he spoke, people listened. He was concerned about America's troubles both at home and abroad and wanted to do all he could to right any injustices he encountered. In print and in public he became a campaigner for social change.

Twain knew that 1900 was a political year and he used his popularity to attack anyone he thought deserved it. No cause he championed was considered too small. When his housekeeper, Katie Leary, was grossly overcharged for a cab fare, Twain took the matter to court. Overcharging by taxi drivers was just something New Yorkers put up with—no one bothered to take them court except Twain. When he won the case, and the driver's taxi license was suspended, the incident received wide publicity.

In the *North American Review* of February 1901 Twain wrote the lead article, entitled "To the Person Sitting in Darkness." It was an attack on American imperialism and social injustices that were occurring without challenge in America and around the world. In it, he denounced the U.S. policies in Africa, China, and the Philippines. Twain used clippings he had seen in the New York *Tribune* and *Sun* newspapers as evidence of the news he commented on. He also commented about crime-ridden areas of New York City where the police would not go.

The article created a whirlwind of reaction. Letters poured in, pro and con. Every major newspaper in England and the United States commented on it. Mark Twain was back, and he wasn't kidding around. One prominent American hailed

To the Person Sitting in Darkness

Twain's satirical North American Review *article of 1901, as reprinted in* The Family Mark Twain, *told about native people who, upon being contacted by American and other missionaries, might have been better off left alone:*

"Shall we go on conferring our Civilization upon the peoples that sit in darkness, or shall we give those poor things a rest? Shall we bang right ahead in our old-time, loud, pious way, and commit the new century to the game; or shall we sober up and sit down and think it over first? Would it not be prudent to get our Civilization tools together, and see how much stock is left on hand in the way of Glass Beads and Theology, and Maxim [machine] Guns and Hymn Books, and Trade Gin and Torches of Progress and Enlightenment (patent adjustable ones, good to fire villages with, upon occasion), and balance the books, and arrive at the profit and loss, so that we may intelligently decide whether to continue the business or sell out the property and start a new Civilization Scheme on the proceeds?

Extending the Blessings of Civilization to our Brother who Sits in Darkness has been a good trade and has paid well, on the whole; and there is money in it yet, if carefully worked—but not enough, in my judgment, to make any considerable risk advisable. . . . Most of those People that Sit in Darkness have been furnished with more light than was good for them or profitable for us. We have been injudicious."

him as "the Voltaire of America." A critic joked, "Please excuse seeming impertinence, but were you ever adjudged insane? Be honest. How much money does the devil give you for arraigning Christianity and missionary causes?"[56] Prominent Englishman Sir Hiram Maxim wrote:

I give you my candid opinion that what you have done is of very great value to the civilization of the world. There is no man living whose words carry greater weight than your own, as no one's writings are so eagerly sought after by the classes.[57]

Commenting in his notebook on the uproar, Twain wrote, "Do right and you will be conspicuous."[58]

In this period Twain wrote mostly essays and articles. He could now afford to write whatever he wanted, and every major periodical was happy to give him a forum. He wanted to use his time for social reformation.

He used his time well. When he spoke

or wrote about politics, for example, people paid close attention. The Tammany Hall group ruled New York politics in those days, and their corruption was quite well-known. Twain supported Tammany opponent and Columbia University president Seth Low, of the Fusion party, for mayor. Twain's speech of October 17, 1900, at the Acorn Society condemned the Tammany candidate and the Tammany boss, Richard Croker. The speech was quoted far and wide, and Tammany Hall lost the election. Twain was given a good share of the credit; one newspaper said his speech turned the election.

Twain's social crusades helped bring

A cartoonist portrays the Tammany Hall politicians as a group of vultures. A speech given by Twain was credited with turning the election in favor of the group's opponent.

him new honors and created renewed interest in his other work. In 1901 he was given an honorary degree of doctor of letters by Yale University. The next year he received a similar honor from the University of Missouri. He made his last trip home to Hannibal then. It was perhaps the most emotionally moving journey of his life. A riverboat was named the *Mark Twain* after him, and he spent long hours with boyhood friends—the same friends who had become characters in *Tom Sawyer* and *Huck Finn.*

Fading Lights

Unfortunately, the happy times were not to last. Twain's brother Orion had died in 1897, and Twain took it hard. He felt Orion's death was "unjust," for reasons known only to him. He had not quite begun to realize, perhaps, that he was at the age when one's friends and relatives begin dying off one after the other, in the natural consequence of things.

After Susy's death, and because of Livy's ongoing health problems and Jean's epilepsy, Twain became obsessed with cures of all kinds. In 1899, while still in Europe, he and Livy learned of the healing powers of osteopathy (known then as "the Swedish movements"). Hoping for a cure for Jean and betterment of their own health, they moved for a few months to Sanna, Sweden, where they all had treatments from Heinrick Kellgren.

With his finances recovered Twain once again cast his roving eye toward get-rich-quick schemes, but this time with a view toward health. He began taking something called "plasmon," which was made from skim milk, and proclaimed its benefits broadly to anyone who would listen. He figured to make a fortune with it in America. Of course, this never happened.

On August 12, 1902, Livy became ill at their summer cottage in Maine. She had been in frail health and had suffered from respiratory problems throughout their years together. Now they both thought she would die, but she fought back. They went back to New York, and she seemed to improve. While Livy convalesced, Twain got busy on a new Huck and Tom story but never finished it. It was obvious why at his sixty-seventh birthday dinner. He told the crowd that "a part of me is not present; the larger part, the better part."[59] Namely, Livy, who was sick at home. Her condition was better, then

To keep his mind off his troubles, Twain corresponded with many friends, such as Helen Keller.

worse, for the rest of the year. She would never fully recover.

To make things worse, in December Jean's epilepsy intensified. Clara, the youngest daughter and known for her truthfulness, had to lie to her mother about Jean's condition. Livy was so ill that she was sheltered from any bad news or anything that might upset her. Twain was permitted only a few minutes a day with his wife; the doctors felt he might swear or do something else that would upset Livy. Some days Livy was too ill for any visitors.

The family situation was so disheartening that Twain got little done—no writing to speak of, and all speaking invitations were declined. To try to keep his mind off his troubles, Twain read Sir Walter Scott's novels and corresponded with people he was fond of, such as Helen Keller, who had just published her autobiography, *The Story of My Life.*

In 1903 Twain sold the Hartford mansion at a loss. The family spent that summer at Quarry Farm in Elmira. Twain tried to write whenever he could find peace of mind. Even then it was usually only an article written for a good cause. He wrote "A Dog's Tale" to protest animal experimentation. It was the last thing he would write in his old study.

In October, with hopes that the Italian climate would improve Livy's health, the family sailed for Florence. Unfortunately it was rainy in Florence, and the villa they had taken was not what they had expected. Still, Livy seemed to get better, and Twain managed to get some stories written, such as "The $30,000 Bequest." He also worked on his *Autobiography,* which he realized by now it was a duty to his public to write.

On June 5, 1904, Twain and Jean

Twain was deeply saddened by the death of his wife Olivia—his editor, best friend, and pillar of support for many years.

found a new, better villa that they thought Livy would love. They came back filled with enthusiasm and were overjoyed when Clara told them that Livy was better than she had been for three months. Twain found his wife bright and cheerful and told her about the new house. He remained for forty-five minutes in her room—far past his usual time—but thought she could stand it. "You will come back," she told him, meaning at his usual visiting time, and he replied "Yes, to say good night."[60]

Then he went upstairs and did something unusual. He began playing on the piano and singing "jubilee" songs, or joyous spirituals, like "Swing Low, Sweet Chariot." "He is singing a good-night carol to me," Livy told her nurse.[61] Then, suddenly, she died.

In contrast to young Susy's death, Livy's had been long in coming. Her chronic illness did not keep Twain from chastising himself or making it seem like another unjust circumstance of life. He wrote in his notebook:

> At a quarter past 9 this evening she that was the life of my life passed to the relief & the peace of death after 22 months of unjust & unearned suffering. I first saw her 37 years ago, & now I have looked upon her face for the last time. Oh, so unexpected! . . . I was full of remorse for things done & said in these 34 years of married life that hurt Livy's heart.[62]

Twain returned to America for the burial and was flooded with messages of sympathy from around the world. Still, his friends and family knew that words and flowers were useless. Olivia Langdon had been the light of his life from the time he had seen her picture in a locket, so long before. She had been his editor, his financier at times, his best friend in all the world. Throughout his troubles, despite her physical frailties, she had been his guiding beacon, his irreplaceable pillar of emotional and spiritual support.

His feelings about her were summed up in one line, published that year in his book *The Diary of Adam and Eve*. Adam says, at Eve's grave: "Wheresoever she was, *there* was Heaven."[63] Without Livy beside him, Mark Twain was a person sitting in darkness.

When we think of Mark Twain, we picture him in the white suit that came to be his trademark. What most people do not realize is that he did not regularly wear such suits until 1906. Certainly, this uniform perfectly suited his lion's mane of white hair, thick white mustache, and furry white eyebrows, but most did not see him dress that way until he returned to public life, after Livy had been gone a couple of years.

Another series of family tragedies followed Livy's loss. In July 1904 Jean was riding a horse that collided with a trolley. She was knocked unconscious and had to be confined to bed to recover. On September 1, Twain's sister Pamela died in Greenwich, Connecticut. When the family relocated to New York City in the fall, Clara was still so upset by the strain of Livy's long illness and shock of her death that she became bedridden and required a nurse's constant care for several months.

Pressing On

Mark Twain somehow survived all the other emotional blows that followed the death of his wife and gradually went back to work. He did not produce much at first.

In 1905 he published three pieces in *Harper's* magazine, but none of lasting significance. The best one was the fictional "Eve's Diary"; it was an obvious tribute to Livy. The fiery, crusading social journalist seemed to be fading fast.

By the time Twain was almost seventy, Clara and Jean had recovered. The family's life now, at 21 Fifth Avenue, was much happier and quite busy. Twain hired a private secretary to help deal with endless social invitations and the constant callers at his home. The visitors were mostly newspaper reporters, since Twain was always good for a quotable opinion. In private conversations and letters, however, he was often glum. Livy was still on his mind: he wrote his niece about a dream in which

Twain's trademark white suit was a perfect complement to his mane of white hair, white bushy eyebrows, and thick white mustache.

Mark Twain on Lying

Reporters knew that Mark Twain was always good for a story. Here is an example, from an interview in the New York Herald *of October 16, 1900, and as taken from Samuel C. Webster's* Mark Twain, Business Man:

"Fate has its revenge on the humorist. Now, I have lied so much, in a genial, good-natured way, of course, that people won't believe me when I speak the truth. . . . It is no longer appreciated—in me. . . . I have, therefore, been forced by fate to adopt fiction as a medium of truth. Most liars lie for the love of the lie; I lie for the love of the truth. I disseminate my true views by means of a series of apparently humorous and mendacious [false, but not misleading] stories. . . . If any man can do that, and finds that he can disseminate facts through the medium of falsehood, he should never speak the truth—and I don't."

Livy visited him, and the sadness he felt when he awoke.

In addition, several of his oldest friends died in 1905. So when talk of a birthday celebration arose, Twain felt there was not much reason to celebrate. He suggested a small gathering over beer and sandwiches with a few friends. Instead, a gala event was organized by Twain's friend, Colonel George Harvey. Invitations went out across America—to his friends and any writer of distinction. Two hundred people gathered on December 5, 1905, in the great room at fashionable Delmonico's restaurant in New York City for a tribute to America's greatest living writer.

The speeches, accolades, and toasts went on for hours. Finally, Twain himself rose and explained to the gathering how he had survived so long. His scheme of living would kill anybody else, he said: he smoked constantly and hated exercise. By the time he closed with a speech, it was early in the morning, and there were tears of joy all around.

The celebration touched Twain deeply and helped him realize just how much he was adored. It also helped boost him above his lingering sorrows. He had published portions of his autobiography in the *North American Review* and *Harper's Weekly* in 1904. Now he saw that the remaining days of his life were numbered and that he owed his public a full-scale version of his life story. Twain made a deal with a young writer, Albert Bigelow Paine, to work on a complete account of his life. It was a wise decision because as his life was coming to a close, his memory was playing tricks on him. (Paine would discover that some of the things Twain recalled were more fiction than fact and needed correction.) Their work continued for the next three years. The world would learn things about Mark Twain they had never known and see that his life itself was a work of art.

Chapter

9 The Most Conspicuous Person on Earth

Many of Twain's last works were not published until well after his death. This was his desire because of the backlash he felt might result. Although many of the theories expressed in these writings seem quaint and scarcely controversial in today's world, the world Mark Twain lived in was quite different. In the day before television or radio, people got their emotional and intellectual stimulation from newspapers and books, and theatrical and social occasions. Sir Hiram Maxim had not been wrong when he told Twain that no man's words carried greater weight. Twain knew the truth of that statement, just as he knew he was going to die before many more years. In his waning years, no matter how he felt, he remained busy, dictating to Paine, speaking where he thought it would matter, and writing continuously—pouring out his deepest feelings for his own generation and those to come.

The Last Public Appearances

Among his other social causes, Mark Twain was dedicated to racial equality. In the winter of 1906 he spoke at Carnegie

Despite failing health, Twain spent countless hours putting the details of his life and his deepest emotions on paper.

Twain's childhood exposure to prejudice probably played an important role in his dedication to racial equality.

Hall to help raise money for black educator Booker T. Washington. The auditorium was filled with celebrities, and Twain seized the opportunity. He said that average Americans were Christians 363 days a year, but when they went to the tax office and the voting booth on the other two days, they left their Christian principles at home and ruined all their good works. The speech had its desired effect, and contributions flowed in.

Twain's political activities were fairly limited because of failing health and a desire to sum up his life in print. He took time to lobby in Washington, however, for better copyright protection. The speaker of the House gave him a private office (and his own butler), and Twain made the best of the opportunity. In a couple of years, a bill was passed that protected generations of writers to come.

Rather than rely on notes for the dozen or so speeches he made in New York that winter, Twain made up his speeches as he went along, inspired by the moment. He was the most popular speaker in the country and known in newspapers as "the belle of New York." The *Evening Mail* described it this way:

> Things have reached the point where, if Mark Twain is not at a public meeting or banquet, he is expected to console it with one of his inimitable letters of advice and encouragement. If he deigns to make a public appearance there is a throng at the doors which overtaxes the energy and ability of the police. We must be glad that we have a public commentator like Mark Twain always at hand and his wit and wisdom continually on tap. His sound, breezy Mississippi Valley Americanism is a corrective to all sorts of snobbery. He cultivates respect for human rights by always making sure that he has his own.[64]

Controversies and Good Byes

Twain did not always receive public praise in his last years. Saying that *Tom Sawyer* and *Huckleberry Finn* posed a threat to children's morals, a librarian in Brooklyn banned the books. When news of this reached the press, word quickly spread across the country, providing free advertising and renewed interest in the novels. Twain laughed the incident off.

On April 19, 1906, Twain gave a farewell lecture at Carnegie Hall to benefit the Robert Fulton Memorial Association. The band played "America" as he took the stage. The great San Francisco earthquake had occurred just the day before, and

"Roasted" by Mark Twain

Twain rarely missed an opportunity to publicly lampoon [poke fun at] an old friend. The following is an excerpt, taken from Paine's biography, from Twain's speech at the Engineer's Club in New York City, in the fall of 1907, about U.S. Steel founder Andrew Carnegie:

"I am going to vary the complimentary monotony. While we have all been listening to the complimentary talk Mr. Carnegie's face has scintillated with fictitious innocence. You'd think he never committed a crime in his life. But he has.

Look at his pestiferous simplified spelling. Imagine the calamity on two sides of the ocean when he foisted his simplified spelling on the whole human race. We've got it all now so that nobody could spell. . . .

If Mr. Carnegie had left spelling alone we wouldn't have had any spots on the sun, or any San Francisco quake, or any business depression.

There, I trust he feels better now and that he has enjoyed my abuse more than he did his compliments. And now that I have him smoothed down and feeling comfortable I just want to say one thing more—that his simplified spelling is all right enough, but, like chastity, you can carry it too far."

U.S. Steel founder Andrew Carnegie, a friend of Twain's.

Twain put in a plea for help for the stricken city. This was followed by a joking history of Fulton, the inventor of the steamboat. Then he retold many of the tales from his last world tour. Twain had invited his biographer along for the occasion, and Paine later reported that applause in the packed house was so frequent that Twain's voice was often drowned out. No one seemed to care. The audience was happy to simply *see* Mark Twain. It turned out not to be his last public lecture, but the audience thought it would be. They calculated they were witnessing a memorable close to an amazing stage career and expressed themselves accordingly.

Dealing with the Public

Just as in Hartford, people from all walks of life made their way to Mark Twain's residence at 21 Fifth Avenue. Most of the time his secretary would explain that Twain could not see them. When Twain sensed the callers were sincere and not overbearing, it was a different story. One young woman merely wanted to sit face to face with him; he interrupted his dictation to Paine and spoke with her for some time.

If Twain was playing billiards—his favorite game—he was more accommodating to visitors. One day this backfired. Mrs. Henry Huddleston Rogers had given Twain a spectacular billiard table, and he and Paine often played while talking over Twain's life. A young man Twain had met and told to "drop in some day" showed up and stayed for hours, talking incessantly about Twain books he had read, the people he had met who knew Twain, and so forth. When the visitor finally left, Twain had to sing an old hymn loudly to rid himself of his accumulated anger.

Twain's mailbox was usually full, but the letters were predictable. Some people sent unsolicited manuscripts to be critiqued. One woman whom he did not know wrote so often that he remarked that she intended to pursue him to the grave. Other writers were helpful, offering advice for his bronchitis and rheumatism. When someone wrote a note of sincere, well-expressed praise, it might make his day. "I can live for two months on a good compliment," he told Paine.[65]

Paine discovered just how true this statement was and how much Mark Twain loved his fans. When they took regular Sunday walks together along Fifth Avenue, Paine quickly realized they were timed to coincide with the neighborhood churches letting out. In his white suit Twain was unmistakable in any crowd. He adored the throngs who showered compliments upon him as he walked along slowly. It was their chance to express gratitude for all that he had given them, and he gloried in their praises.

A Man of Letters

When he was not dictating his biography to Paine and their stenographer, Mrs. Hobby, Twain wrote continuously. He published his book *Adam's Diary* (a satirical account of the Garden of Eden) in 1904. In

Twain's New York residence, where he was bombarded by drop-in visitors and a flood of fan mail.

1905 he gave numerous speeches and published a number of articles in *Harper's New Monthly*. In 1906, his small book *What Is Man?* was privately printed and distributed because Twain did not want to upset his broad audience with the book's darker philosophies. In 1905 he wrote *The War Prayer*. In it a church congregation gathers to pray to God for their soldiers marching off to war. Into the church walks an "aged stranger" who extends the prayer into the inevitable consequences of war that the worshipers do not want to confront. The stranger describes what they are *really* praying for, in no uncertain terms:

> O Lord Our God, help us to tear their soldiers to bloody shreds with our shells; help us to cover their smiling fields with the pale forms of their patriot dead; help us to drown the thunder of the guns with the shrieks of their wounded writhing in pain; help us to lay waste their humble homes with a hurricane of fire; help us to wring the hearts of their unoffending widows with unavailing grief; help us to turn them out rootless with their little children to wander unfriended the wastes of their desolated land, in rags and hunger and thirst.[66]

And on and on, until at the end the congregation thinks the "aged stranger was a lunatic," and "there was no sense in what he said."

In this day of televised graphic violence of wars around the world, we can see the truth of *The War Prayer*. Twain told his friend Dan Beard that "only dead men can tell the truth" and would not let the book be published until after his death. His daughter Jean agreed, saying that *The*

Twain's biographer Albert Bigelow Paine worked tirelessly to sort out fiction and reality from Twain's verbal account of his life.

War Prayer would be considered sacrilege.

As Paine worked on Twain's biography, he discovered that Twain told the truth the way Huck Finn did—"mainly." Twain had used his imagination so intensely over the years that he sometimes innocently confused his own mental creations with memory. But Paine was able to sort out fiction from reality. He became Twain's constant companion until his death and put together a remarkable four-volume work on the great writer's life. The biography provides a remarkable insight into Twain's life and work, and Paine worked tirelessly getting the details correct. Among other things, he traveled to the West Coast and interviewed Twain's old friends, including a dying Steve Gillis.

Paine became the coexecutor of Twain's literary estate, along with Clara Clemens Gabrilowitch, Twain's daughter. After Twain's death one of his last great works, *The Mysterious Stranger*, was edited by Paine from four different versions into the one most commonly available today. Twain chose several different settings and dates for the story; Paine settled on the one set in Austria in 1590. The stranger—whom Twain named Satan—tells the hero that the human race lives a "life of continuous and uninterrupted self-deception." At the end of the tale, Satan says:

> There is no God, no universe, no human race, no earthly life, no heaven, no hell. It is all a dream—a grotesque and foolish dream. Nothing exists but

you. And you are but a *thought*—a vagrant thought, a useless thought, a homeless thought, wandering forlorn among the empty eternities! [67]

Just as these statements are generally considered false, we must remember that Twain did not try to resolve the story and publish it before his death. Perhaps he never intended it to be published at all. The fact is, he *did* believe in God, in a life beyond this one, and in spiritual matters in general. His confusion was mostly over how to gain certainty about such things.

In 1907 Twain was given a doctorate of letters degree by Oxford University. His four weeks in England can only be compared to the commotion created by the Beatles when they arrived in the United States in 1964. When ten thousand English fans showed up to see one Twain lecture, the police did not open the doors in

---

A Curious Correspondence

One man wrote Twain claiming he wished he had never read his books, but not saying why. Twain showed the letter to a reporter, who printed it in the paper. Another letter followed; it is taken from Paine's biography:

"My Dear Sir—I saw in to-day's paper a copy of the letter which I wrote you October 26th.

I have read and re-read your works until I can almost recall some of them word for word. My familiarity with them is a constant source of pleasure which I would not have missed, and therefore the regret which I have expressed is more than offset by thankfulness.

Believe me, the regret which I feel for having read your works is entirely due to the unalterable fact that I can never again have the pleasure of reading them for the first time.

Your sincere admirer,
George B. Lauder"

time. There was a stampede that broke down doors and resulted in injuries. At a garden party given by English royalty at Windsor Castle, with Twain as the foremost guest, eighty-five hundred notables attended. It seemed that every movement Twain made in England became headlines.

Twain and English playwright George Bernard Shaw greatly admired each other's work. When they met during Twain's last visit to England, Shaw gave him the following note:

> I am persuaded that the future historian of America will find your works as indispensable to him as a French historian finds the political tracts of Voltaire. I tell you so because I am the author of a play in which a priest says, "Telling the truth's the funniest joke

An artist depicts Twain visiting with English royalty during a garden party at Windsor Castle.

in the world," a piece of wisdom which you helped to teach me.[68]

In addition to his travels and the ongoing dictation of his biography, Twain published two books that year. *Christian Science* was intended to be a humorous look at what Twain thought was the next big religion. (Although Twain publicly joked about the religion's founder, Mary Baker Eddy, he privately admired her.) *Captain Stormfield's Visit to Heaven* was a comic look at the traditional Christian view of Heaven. It was the last book published during his lifetime and exhibited the old Mark Twain humor that the public so dearly loved.

When Albert Bigelow Paine died in 1937, there were still thousands of pages of unpublished Mark Twain writings. Twain's daughter Clara would not allow the publication of *Letters from the Earth* until 1939. In it, "Satan" writes letters to heaven, explaining what the human race is doing on earth. A good bit of the book is Mark Twain's mental wrestling with religion, philosophy, and his depression over the low points of humanity. He describes earth, for example:

> The people are all insane, the other animals are all insane, the earth is insane, Nature itself is insane. Man is a marvelous curiosity. When he is at his very very best he is a sort of low grade nickel-plated angel; at his worst he is unspeakable, unimaginable; and first and last and all the time he is a sarcasm. Yet he blandly and in all sincerity calls himself the "noblest work of God.". . . I must put one more strain upon you: he thinks he is going to heaven![69]

Again, this is the depressed Mark Twain, the gloomy Mark Twain, not the Mark

Twain and his daughter Clara became very close during his final years.

sion as it departed from his new hilltop home in Redding, Connecticut.

Twain later reported to Paine that he went into his "always warm" bathroom after Jean's procession left. He closed the door, and

> All at once I felt a cold current of air about me. I thought the door must be open; but it was closed. I said "Jean, is this you trying to let me know you have found the others?" Then the cold air was gone.[70]

Experiences like this do not come to a man who believes that "it is all a dream." The day after Jean's death Stormfield—Twain's home in Redding—was engulfed in a snowstorm. Twain remarked: "Jean always so loved to see a storm like this, and just now at Elmira they are burying her."[71] It was another magical, if coincidental, happening in the life of Mark Twain, and he was compelled to write about it. "The Death of Jean" was published in *Harper's New Monthly*, in December 1910. It was the last thing Twain sold for publication.

Twain who made a world laugh. It is fitting that he did not publish *Letters* or even want it published. Even more to the point, he wrote it in 1909. That was the year of his daughter Jean's death; he had suffered the loss of many other dear friends and relatives as well.

The Death of Jean

Jean died of an epileptic seizure just before Christmas, and the funeral was held during a snowfall on Christmas Day. Clara had married the Russian pianist Ossip Gabrilowitch, and they were honeymooning in Europe. They came back in time for the funeral, but Twain was too ill to attend. He could only watch the sad proces-

Out with the Comet

Over the next few months, Twain spent a good deal of time in Bermuda to help ease a heart condition that had been worsening since 1907. When it was obvious he was dying, Paine went there and brought him back to Stormfield. On April 20, 1910, Halley's Comet was once again in the skies over America. The next day Mark Twain looked up from his bed and told his daughter, Clara, "Good-by. If we meet. . . ."[72] Then he was gone from this life. True to his prediction, he had come in

The Truth About Angels

In Captain Storm-field's Visit to Heaven, *the title character is told that things in paradise don't work quite the way he expected, particularly with regard to angels:*

"*You* ain't built for wings—no man is. You know what a grist of years it took you to come here from the earth—and yet you were booming along faster than any cannon-ball could go. Suppose you had to fly that distance with your wings—wouldn't eternity have been over before you got here? Certainly. Well, angels have to go to the earth every day—millions of them—to appear in visions to dying children and good people, you know—it's the heft [weight] of their business. They appear with their wings, of course, because they are on official service, and because the dying persons wouldn't know they were angels if they hadn't wings—but do you reckon they fly with them? It stands to reason they don't. The wings would wear out before they got half-way; even the pinfeathers would be gone; the wing frames would be as bare as kite sticks before the paper is pasted on. The distances in heaven are billions of times greater; angels have to go all over heaven every day; could they do it with wings alone? No, indeed; they wear the wings for style, but they travel any distance in an instant by *wishing*. The wishing-carpet of the Arabian Nights was a sensible idea—but our earthly ideas of angels flying these awful distances with their clumsy wings was foolish."

Twain appears ravaged by old age and failing health in this photograph, taken near the time of his death.

with the comet, and gone out with it, too, seventy-five years later.

At the funeral at New York's Brick Church, thousands filed past his casket for one last look at the greatest celebrity America had ever given the world. He was buried in Elmira with the rest of his family. Fittingly, it rained that day. The skies were sullen and dark, and the quiet, steady downpour continued all afternoon.

Stormfield—Twain's home in Redding, Connecticut. It was in this house that the literary genius spent the final moments of his life.

Paine described the tributes which followed:

> It is not so often that a whole world mourns. . . . Let us only say that it was because he was so limitlessly human that every other human heart, in whatever sphere or circumstance, responded to his touch. From every remote corner of the globe the cables of condolence swept in; every printed sheet in Christendom was filled with lavish tribute; pulpits forgot his heresies and paid him honor. No king ever died that received so rich a homage as his. To quote or to individualize would be to cheapen this vast offering.[73]

And so the great man passed from this life. He had warmed the world with his humor and wit and shaken apart public injustice with the written word. He had intellectually examined taboo subjects and had the audacity to write his deepest feelings on them. Though he was gone from the flesh, the body of literature he left behind was an immense legacy. In retrospect, even the decisions to publish certain works only after his death were strokes of genius. Justin Kaplan said it best in 1974:

> The reputation and popularity of Mark Twain have never stood higher than they do now. At no time since his death have his work and spirit seemed quite so apt, so welcome, so contemporary. His strategy of "speaking from the grave" displayed with good reason, "the calm confidence of a Christian with four aces."[74]

Mark Twain's Legacy

To understand the contributions that Mark Twain made to world society and literature, it is necessary to comprehend what the United States went through during his lifetime. During the seventy-five years that Samuel Clemens lived, America defined itself to the world and became the most influential nation. Mark Twain, through his writings, gave definition to what it meant to be American.

When Sam Clemens was a river pilot, white civilization—large cities that had police forces and cultural establishments like museums and operas—stopped at the eastern bank of the Mississippi River. California, on the West Coast, had been settled for centuries—since the time of the Spanish land grants—but there was a huge area of land between California and the Mississippi that was considered open for the taking.

Western expansion brought about a whole new way of life. Vast fortunes were made when poor men found gold, silver, and other valuable ores. There were marshals and sheriffs, but scarcely enough to go around. Often enough, the person who shot quickest and most accurately made the rules. Life was generally a rough and tumble scramble "out West." And Mark Twain became the voice of the western frontier. Later he served as an international example of the American spirit.

Sam Clemens was a student of people and speech throughout his life. As such he made constant mental and written notes regarding the customs and speech of western Americans and reported them faithfully in his works. As explained in the Public Broadcasting System television series and accompanying book, *The Story of*

For the generations of readers who have read and enjoyed his writings, and for the generations to come, the legacy of Mark Twain continues.

A theater advertises a stage version of Twain's A Connecticut Yankee in King Arthur's Court *in 1922. Even today, new versions of Twain's stories still pop up in film and in print.*

English, many of the slang phrases we now take for granted first appeared in the writings of Mark Twain. For example, in his book *Roughing It*, Twain explains that the word *heap* is "Injun-English" for *very much*. *Dead broke, take it easy, to get even, gilt-edged*, and *a close call* were all introduced to the American public by Twain. As poet T.S. Eliot described it, Mark Twain was

> one of those writers, of whom there are not a great many in literature, who have discovered a new way of writing, valid not only for themselves but for others. I should place him . . . as one of those rare writers who have brought their language up to date.[75]

Mark Twain brought all the color of the expanding United States and its "new" English to the world through his writings and public appearances. It is doubtful that he set out intentionally to create such an effect, but things had a way of working out for Sam Clemens, despite occasional obstacles.

Mark Twain's influence on American society continues. New versions of Twain stories inevitably pop up each year, in Hollywood or in print. The 1990s television series "Star Trek: The Next Generation" featured an episode where Captain Picard goes back in time to San Francisco and brings Mark Twain back to the spaceship. The cover of the November 1992 issue of *GQ* magazine was of presidential candidate Bill Clinton and his running mate, Al Gore. The main article, mentioned on the cover, was by Gore Vidal: "Huck and Tom" said the cover. In 1993 yet another film version of *The Adventures of Huckleberry Finn* was released.

Will the interest ever stop? Probably not, as long as there are readers and people who love to laugh. Above everything else, Mark Twain made people laugh, but he made them think, too. When his words still do the trick, over a hundred years later, it is safe to say he is immortal. Or, as he told a newsman who was investigating a rumor that he had died:

> "Reports of my death were greatly exaggerated."[76]

Notes

Chapter 1: In with the Comet

1. Justin Kaplan, *Mark Twain and His World.* New York: Simon & Schuster, 1974. Reprint. New York: Harmony Books, 1982.

2. Kaplan, *Mark Twain and His World.*

3. Albert Bigelow Paine, *Mark Twain, A Biography: The Personal and Literary Life of Samuel Langhorne Clemens.* New York and London: Harper & Brothers, 1912.

4. Mark Twain, *Life on the Mississippi.* New York: Harper & Brothers, 1906.

5. Kaplan, *Mark Twain and His World.*

6. Paine, *Mark Twain, A Biography*, vol. 1.

7. Kaplan, *Mark Twain and His World.*

Chapter 2: Life on the Mississippi

8. Samuel Clemens, letter to Pamela Clemens Moffett, 1853. Mark Twain papers, University of California, Berkeley.

9. Paine, *Mark Twain, A Biography*, vol. 1.

10. Samuel Clemens, letter to Pamela Clemens Moffett, December 5, 1853. Mark Twain papers, University of California, Berkeley.

11. Mark Twain, "The Turning Point of My Life," *Harper's Bazaar*, February 1910.

12. Twain, *Life on the Mississippi.*

13. Twain, *Life on the Mississippi.*

14. Paine, *Mark Twain, A Biography*, vol. 1.

15. Paine, *Mark Twain, A Biography*, vol. 2.

16. Samuel C. Webster, ed., *Mark Twain, Business Man.* Boston: Little, Brown, 1946.

17. Webster, *Mark Twain, Business Man.*

Chapter 3: Roughing It

18. Mark Twain, *Roughing It.* New York: Harper & Row, 1913.

19. Judge A.W. (Gus) Oliver to Albert Bigelow Paine, *Mark Twain, A Biography*, vol. 1.

20. William R. Gillis, *Gold Rush Days with Mark Twain.* New York: Albert & Charles Boni, 1930.

21. Ivan Benson, *Mark Twain's Western Years.* Palo Alto, CA: Stanford University Press, 1938.

22. As told by Steve Gillis to Albert Bigelow Paine, *Mark Twain, A Biography*, vol. 1.

Chapter 4: Travels to Enchanted Lands

23. Paine, *Mark Twain, A Biography*, vol. 1.

24. Nigey Lennon, *Mark Twain in California: The Turbulent California Years of Samuel Clemens.* San Francisco: Chronicle Books, 1982.

25. Lennon, *Mark Twain in California.*

26. Paine, *Mark Twain, A Biography*, vol. 1.

27. Dixon Wecter, ed., *Mark Twain to Mrs. Fairbanks* (letter collection). San Marino, CA: Huntington Library, 1949.

28. Paine, *Mark Twain, A Biography*, vol. 1.

29. Paine, *Mark Twain, A Biography*, vol. 1.

30. Paine, *Mark Twain, A Biography*, vol. 1.

Chapter 5: The Gilded Age

31. Kaplan, *Mark Twain and His World.*

32. Paine, *Mark Twain, A Biography*, vol. 2.

33. Robert McCrum, William Cran, and Robert MacNeil, *The Story of English.* New York: Elisabeth Sifton Books-Viking, 1986.

34. *America's Historic Places: An Illustrated Guide to Our Country's Past.* Pleasantville, NY: Reader's Digest Association, 1988.

35. Paine, *Mark Twain, A Biography*, vol. 1.

36. Paine, *Mark Twain, A Biography*, vol. 2.

37. Paine, *Mark Twain, A Biography*, vol. 2.

38. Paine, *Mark Twain, A Biography*, vol. 2.

Chapter 6: Philosopher and Publisher

39. Paine, *Mark Twain, A Biography*, vol. 2.

40. Paine, *Mark Twain, A Biography*, vol. 2.

41. Paine, *Mark Twain, A Biography*, vol. 2.

42. Paine, *Mark Twain, A Biography*, vol. 2.

43. Paine, *Mark Twain, A Biography*, vol. 2.

44. Samuel Clemens, letter to Pamela Clemens Moffett, February 7, 1868. Mark Twain papers.

45. Roy Harvey Pearce, "Yours Truly, Huck Finn," *Modern Critical Views: Mark Twain*. New York: Chelsea House Publishers, 1986.

46. Paine, *Mark Twain, A Biography*, vol. 2.

Chapter 7: A Connecticut Yankee's Misfortunes

47. Paine, *Mark Twain, A Biography*, vol. 3.

48. Paine, *Mark Twain, A Biography*, vol. 3.

49. Rudyard Kipling, "Rudyard Kipling on Mark Twain," *New York Herald*, August 17, 1890.

50. Mark Twain, *Personal Recollections of Joan of Arc*. New York: Harper & Row, 1896.

51. Dixon Wecter, editor, *The Love Letters of Mark Twain*. New York: Harper & Brothers, 1949.

52. Paine, *Mark Twain, A Biography*, vol. 3.

53. Paine, *Mark Twain, A Biography*, vol. 3.

Chapter 8: To a Person Sitting in Darkness

54. Paine, *Mark Twain, A Biography*, vol. 3.

55. Clifton Daniel, editorial director, *Chronicle of America*. Mount Kisco, NY: Chronicle Publications, 1989.

56. Paine, *Mark Twain, A Biography*, vol. 3.

57. Paine, *Mark Twain, A Biography*, vol. 3.

58. Paine, *Mark Twain, A Biography*, vol. 3.

59. Paine, *Mark Twain, A Biography*, vol. 3.

60. Paine, *Mark Twain, A Biography*, vol. 3.

61. Paine, *Mark Twain, A Biography*, vol. 3.

62. Paine, *Mark Twain, A Biography*, vol. 3.

63. Mark Twain, *The Diary of Adam and Eve*.

Chapter 9: The Most Conspicuous Person on Earth

64. Paine, *Mark Twain, A Biography*, vol. 4.

65. Paine, *Mark Twain, A Biography*, vol. 4.

66. Mark Twain, *The War Prayer*. New York: Harper & Row, 1923.

67. Mark Twain, *The Mysterious Stranger and Other Stories*. New York: Harper & Row, 1922.

68. Paine, *Mark Twain, A Biography*, vol. 4.

69. Mark Twain, *Letters from the Earth*. Ed. Bernard De Voto. New York: Harper & Row, 1959.

70. Paine, *Mark Twain, A Biography*, vol. 4.

71. Paine, *Mark Twain, A Biography*, vol. 4.

72. Paine, *Mark Twain, A Biography*, vol. 4.

73. Paine, *Mark Twain, A Biography*, vol. 4.

74. Kaplan, *Mark Twain and His World*.

Epilogue: Mark Twain's Legacy

75. McCrum, Cran, and MacNeil, *The Story of English*.

76. Mark Twain papers.

For Further Reading

Author's note: The life and works of Mark Twain have been written about by scholars around the world. Check with your local library for Twain's books and stories and books about him. Some of his best works are listed below, as well as places to find more information about one of America's most famous authors. Many of Twain's novels have been made into films or television programs. Huckleberry Finn has been the subject of several movies and a Broadway musical. Check your local library or video store.

Books and Stories by Twain

The Adventures of Huckleberry Finn is possibly the best children's novel ever written. It examines social issues that remain controversial even today. It is funny and remarkable for the way the main character, Huck, tells the story in the Missouri dialect of his day.

The Adventures of Tom Sawyer is a classic story of a boy growing up in a Missouri river town. Tom plays pranks, falls in love, and is chased by a murderer. He and his friend Huckleberry Finn even witness their own funeral. *Tom Sawyer Abroad* and *Tom Sawyer, Detective* provide further adventures of Tom.

A Connecticut Yankee in King Arthur's Court caused an uproar in England when first published because it makes fun of royalty everywhere. It tells the story of an American inventor named Hank Morgan who travels through time to ancient England and gets into all sorts of trouble.

The Diary of Adam and Eve is a humorous retelling of the Garden of Eden story. The concluding sentiment that Adam expresses toward Eve is really Twain speaking of his wife, Olivia.

"The Notorious Jumping Frog of Calaveras County," about a man who loses a bet about a frog jumping contest, is the story that made Twain nationally famous.

The Prince and the Pauper is Twain's most charming tale, about two look-alikes—a poor boy of London and the crown prince of England—who switch places and risk losing everything.

The War Prayer is a dark, haunting tale written toward the end of Twain's life, about the true nature of war.

Sources of Information

In addition to the works listed above, the following sources provide additional information on Mark Twain.

The Mark Twain Papers collection at the University of California, Berkeley, is the best source of letters written by and to Twain, newspaper clippings pertaining to his life and work, and Twain memorabilia.

The Mark Twain Society, Box 3225, Elmira, NY 14905, publishes a regular newsletter and is a fine source of information. Membership fee is $5.

Works Consulted

Ivan Benson, *Mark Twain's Western Years.* Palo Alto, CA: Stanford University Press, 1938. This book describes a period of Twain's life that is not well known and provides much insight into how he helped bring America's West and East together through his stories.

Justin Kaplan, *Mark Twain and His World.* New York: Simon & Schuster, 1974. Reprint. New York: Harmony Books, 1982. Justin Kaplan is one of the foremost Mark Twain scholars and has written several books about Twain, all worth reading. This book covers Twain's entire life in 213 pages.

Nigey Lennon, *Mark Twain in California: The Turbulent California Years of Samuel Clemens.* San Francisco: Chronicle Books, 1982. Mark Twain's California years were formative in the development of his career. The book covers his friendship with fellow author Bret Harte, how his skill as a lecturer began, and possible early love interests.

Albert Bigelow Paine, *Mark Twain, A Biography: The Personal and Literary Life of Samuel Langhorne Clemens.* New York and London: Harper & Brothers, 1912. This is the biography Mark Twain authorized and dictated. It is often hard to find, but a must read for serious Twain enthusiasts, for all Twain biographers after Paine have consulted this work. It exists in a three-volume set and a rarer four-volume edition. The four-volume version runs almost eighteen hundred pages. It includes rare photographs, lecture posters, letters, newspaper articles by Twain, and the text of some of Twain's most memorable speeches.

Mark Twain, Ed. Bernard De Voto, *Letters from the Earth.* New York: Harper & Row, 1959. De Voto developed almost an entire career by finding and editing unpublished Twain stories. This collection contains stories that Twain would not allow to be published during his lifetime because of their subject matter, although they seem relatively harmless today.

Mark Twain, *Life on the Mississippi.* New York: Harper & Brothers, 1906. To fully understand Twain's life as a river pilot and the great inspiration it provided throughout his life, this book is a must read. The description of dawn on the Mississippi is wonderful.

Mark Twain, *Roughing It.* New York: Harper & Row, 1913. In this humorous book Twain retells his adventures in the West, though not always as events really happened. This book is where many western phrases that are now a regular part of our language first appeared before a national audience.

Additional Works Consulted

America's Historic Places: An Illustrated Guide to Our Country's Past. Pleasantville, NY: Reader's Digest Association, 1988.

Samuel Clemens, letter to Orion Clemens, October 26, 1853; Samuel Clemens, letter to Pamela Clemens Moffett, 1853, Mark Twain papers.

Clifton Daniel, editorial director, *Chronicle of America*. Mount Kisco, NY: Chronicle Publications, 1989.

William R. Gillis, *Gold Rush Days with Mark Twain*. New York: Albert & Charles Boni, 1930.

Rudyard Kipling, "Rudyard Kipling on Mark Twain," *New York Herald*, August 17, 1890.

Robert McCrum, William Cran, and Robert MacNeil, *The Story of English*. New York: Elisabeth Sifton Books-Viking, 1986.

Charles Neider, *Papa, An Intimate Biography of Mark Twain by His Thirteen-year-old Daughter Susy*. Garden City, NY: Doubleday & Company, Inc., 1985.

Roy Harvey Pearce, "Yours Truly, Huck Finn," *Modern Critical Views: Mark Twain*. New York: Chelsea House Publishers, 1986.

Mark Twain, *The American Claimant*. Hartford, CT: Charles Webster and Co., 1892.

Mark Twain, *Captain Stormfield's Visit to Heaven*. New York: Harper & Brothers, 1909.

Mark Twain, *The Mysterious Stranger and Other Stories*. New York: Harper & Row, 1922.

Mark Twain, *Personal Recollections of Joan of Arc*. New York: Harper & Row, 1896.

Mark Twain, "To the Person Sitting in Darkness," reprinted in *The Family Mark Twain*. New York: Dorset Press, 1988.

Mark Twain, "The Turning Point of My Life," *Harper's Bazaar*, February 1910.

Mark Twain, *The War Prayer*. New York: Harper & Row, 1923.

Samuel C. Webster, editor, *Mark Twain, Business Man*. Boston: Little, Brown, 1946.

Dixon Wecter, editor, *The Love Letters of Mark Twain*. New York: Harper & Brothers, 1949.

Owen Wister, "In Homage to Mark Twain," reprinted in *The Family Mark Twain*. New York: Dorset Press, 1988.

Index

Picture Credits

Cover photo from The Bettmann Archive

The Bettmann Archive, 35, 37, 47, 60, (right), 63, 65, 75, 77, 93

Carnegie Library of Pittsburgh, 92

Culver Pictures, Inc., 7, 12, 15 (bottom), 18, 20, 24, 41, 42, 52, 62, 71, 81, 82, 85, 86, 97, 100

Library of Congress, 8, 9, 11, 13, 15 (top), 29, 39, 44, 51, 54, 57, 59, 60 (center & left), 66, 68, 70, 72, 74, 79, 87, 88, 90, 91, 96, 98, 101

Mark Twain Memorial, Hartford, CT, 55

National Archives, 27, 53

Northwind Picture Archives, 19, 21, 25, 28, 30, 31, 32, 33, 34, 38, 45, 64

UPI/Bettmann, 48, 84, 99

About the Author

Skip Press is an award-winning writer who has received national recognition in almost all forms of media: print, radio, stage, screen, television, and video. In recent years he has published fiction and nonfiction books and magazine articles for young adults. His stories have appeared in such periodicals as *Boy's Life* and *Disney Adventures*.

A Rave of Snakes, the first of his You Solve It young adult mystery series, will be released by Zebra Books in 1994. Press is a member of the Dramatists Guild and other national writing societies and teaches in the UCLA Extension Writer's Program. He lives with his wife Debra, son Haley, and daughter Holly in Burbank, California.